THE MIDDLE AGES

SECOND EDITION

R. J. COOTES

Pearson Education Limited
Edinburgh Gate, Harlow,
Essex CM20 2JE, England
and Associated Companies throughout the world.

Published in the United States of America
by Longman Inc., New York.

First published 1972
Second edition 1989
Sixteenth impression 2005

Set in 11/13 point Plantin (Linotron)
Printed in China.
SWTC/16

ISBN-10: 0-582-31783-5
ISBN-13: 978-0-582-31783-3

British Library Cataloguing in Publication Data

Cootes, R. J.
  The Middle Ages, R. J. Cootes. — 2nd ed. —
  (Longman secondary histories).
  1. Great Britain — History — Anglo-Saxon
  period, 449-1066 2. Great Britain —
  Medieval period, 1066-1485
  I. Title
  942   DA130

  ISBN 0-582-31783-5

Library of Congress Cataloging-in-Publication Data

Cootes, R. J. (Richard John)
  The Middle Ages/R. J. Cootes. — 2nd ed.
  p. cm. — (Longman secondary histories)
  Summary: Describes daily life and major historical events of the Middle
  Ages, with an emphasis on events in Great Britain from the fifth to the
  fifteenth centuries.
  ISBN 0-582-31783-5
  1. Great Britain — History — Medieval period, 1066-1485 — Juvenile
  literature. 2. England — Civilization — Medieval period, 1066-1485 —
  Juvenile literature. 3. Great Britain — History — Anglo-Saxon period,
  449-1066 — Juvenile literature. 4. England — Civilization — To 1066 —
  Juvenile literature. 5. Middle Ages — Juvenile literature.
  [1. Middle Ages. 2. Civilization, Medieval. 3. Great Britain — History —
  Anglo-Saxon period, 449-1066. 4. Great Britain — History — Medieval
  period, 1066-1485.] I. Title. II. Series: Longman secondary histories
  (Unnumbered)
  [DA130.C66 1989]
  942 — dc19

CONTENTS

ACKNOWLEDGEMENTS

We are grateful to Century Hutchinson Publishing Group Ltd for permission to reproduce extracts from *The Later Middle Ages: Portraits and Documents* by D. Baker (published by Hutchinson Education, an imprint of Century Hutchinson Ltd.)

We are grateful to the following for permission to reproduce the following photographs: AA Photo Library, pages 178–9; Abbeville Bibliotheque Muncipale (ET Archive), page 53; Aerofilms, pages 133 *below*, 136, 156, 164, 167; Archive National, Paris (Photographie Giraudon), page 121; Ashmolean Museum, pages 69 *centre*, 82; Britain on View Photographic Library (BTA/ETB), page 198; Barnaby's Picture Library, pages 29 *above*, 44 *above*, 92–3, 181; Bibliotheque Nationale, Paris, page 208; Bibliotheque Royale Albert, page 191; Bodleian Library, Oxford, pages 35, 61 (ET Archive), 110–1, 116–7; British Library, pages 21, 36, 62, 68, 85, 88–9, 120, 124, 128 *above*, 134, 137 *above*, 140, 142, 144, 149 *above*, 166 *above*, 171 *below*, 179, 180, 182 *below right*, 182 *above right*, 182 *below left*, 186, 193, 196, 197 *above*, 197 *below*, 201, 202, 205, 206, 210, 215 *below*, 217 *below*, 218; British Museum, pages 13 *below*, 28, 37, 62–3, 63, 67, 69, *left*, 70, 114, 172 *below*, 192–3; Cambridge University Collection of Air Photographs, page 105; Syndics of Cambridge University Collection, HMSO, page 17; Cambridge University Library, page 214; Camera Press, page 49; Dean & Chapter, Canterbury, page 118–9; J. Allan Cash, pages 43, 123, 160 *below right*, 209; Central Office of Information, page 176; The Governing body of Christ Church Oxford, page 116–7; City Council Museum, Lincoln, page 69 *right* (ET Archive); Crown, Copyright. Controller of Her Majesty's Stationary Office, page 160 *above*; Contemporary Films, page 22 *above*; Master and Fellows. Corpus Christi College, Cambridge, pages 84–5; Corpus Christi College, Oxford, page 110–1; Department of the Environment, HMSO, pages 108, 219; Deutsches Shuh Museum, Offenbach Main, page 177; Fotomas Index, page 122; Fox Photos/Photosource, page 220; John Freeman, pages 91, 92, 93 *below*, 94–5, 96–7; French Government Tourist Office, page 128 *below*; Grand National Archery Society, page 200 *right*, Hereford Dean and Chapter of, pages 138–9; Michael Holford, pages 88, 89, 93 *above*, 96 *below*, 99, 100, 102–3, 160 *below left*; Hulton, pages 138, 169, 204; Hunterian Museum, Glasgow, page 154; The Huntingdon Library, San Marino, California, page 141; International Stock Exchange Photo Library, page 185; Ipswich Museum, page 13 *above*; A. F. Kersting, pages 31, 33, 39, 72, 83, 109 *above*, 112, 118, 126 *below*, 200 *left*; Mansell Collection, pages 22 *below*, 50–1, 106, 117, 130, 147, 148, 150–1, 215 *above*, 217 *above*; The Metropolitan Museum of Art, Gift of George Blumenthal 1941 (41.100.157) page 58; Musee Conde, Chantilly (Photographie Giraudon), pages 25, 26–7, 57; Musee Goya, Castres (Photographie Giraudon), page 56; Musee du Louvre (Photographie Giraudon), pages 52–3; Museum of London, page 178; Museum for Prehistoric Archaeology of Schleswig-Holstein, page 16; The National Museum, Copenhagen, page 77; National Portrait Gallery, London, pages 102, 207; National Museums & Galleries on Merseyside: Liverpool Museum, page 29 *below*; The Order of St. John, page 126 *above*; Photographie Giraudon, page 146; Picturepoint, pages 28–9, 45, 48, 65, 129; Popperfoto, pages 24, 44 *below*, 171 *above*; Public Record Office, London, pages 109 *below*, 211; Royal Commission on the Historical Monuments of England, pages 132–3, 133 *above*, (Rev M. Ridgway), 162, 172 *above*, 213; Royal Danish Ministry for Foreign Affairs, Copenhagen, page 76; Dr J. K. St Joseph, page 79; Scala, page 182 *above left*; Science Museum, London, page 183; *The Scotsman*, pages 32–3; Ronald Sheridan, page 41; Staatsbibliothek, Bamberg, page 54; Stiftsbibliothek, St Gallen, page 60; The Syndics of the Fitzwilliam Museum, Cambridge, page 170; Trinity College, Cambridge, pages 166 centre left, 166 *centre right*, 166 *below left*, 166 *below right*, 190–1; Trinity College Library, University of Dublin, page 187; Universitetets Oldsaksamling, Oslo, page 73; Barbara Wagstaff, page 12; Warburg Institute (Royal Commission on the Historical Monuments of England), page 149 *below*; Weidenfeld & Nicholson, page 127; Woodmansterne, page 145; Reproduced by Gracious permission of Her Majesty The Queen (Royal Library, Windsor Castle), page 152.
Cover: Peasants revolt with banners of England and St. George from the Froissart Chronicles of England and France, 1460–1480. Photo: British Library.

PREFACE

To give this book, wide appeal, great care has been taken to keep the language clear and straightforward. As an aid to clarity, and in the hope of stimulating some genuine interest and understanding, major topics are given a more generous allocation of space than is customary in books of this kind. It is felt that most pupils derive little benefit from a brief, superficial coverage of history.

English history provides the backbone of the book, but outstanding European and Near-Eastern events and personalities have not been ignored. Consequently almost half the chapters are devoted either wholly or partly to developments outside England. Some topics that are often treated separately, including castles, methods of warfare and the development of the English legal system, are here incorporated into chapters with a chronological framework. It is believed that, where possible, social and political aspects should be integrated, to offer the reader 'pegs' to hang things on.

This *second edition* takes account of significant changes in the approach to history teaching since the early 1970s. Frequent attempts to relate the narrative to its sources were a feature of the first edition, but now longer passages are quoted in the text, pictorial evidence is made more explicit, and, above all, extensive documentary work sections have been included. Each of the nine main divisions of the book ends with a collection of documents and questions, and the remaining chapters all have a shorter 'Sources and Questions' section which contains at least one substantial piece of documentary evidence and usually a set of 'picture questions' too.

The many documents in this new edition have been selected on grounds of interest, relevance to the text, and, not least, accessibility to the young reader. All have been carefully edited and glossed to remove barriers to understanding. Original source material is of course not an end in itself. Its function in this book is both to sharpen historical awareness and develop pupils' ability to use and evaluate evidence critically.

I should like to thank Dr Marjorie Reeves, Mr L. E. Snellgrove and my wife, Sarah, for their advice and encouragement.

Richard Cootes

TO THE READER

'The Middle Ages' and 'Medieval'

In studying history it is useful to divide the past into large chunks or 'periods' of time. No doubt you have already come across such terms as *The Ancient World* or *Ancient Times* – the oldest period of man's history, ending with the break-up of the Roman Empire. At the other end of the scale, we call the most recent period of history – the last four or five hundred years – *The Modern Age*.

It follows that the years in between ancient and modern history are called *The Middle Ages*, or *Medieval Times* (the Latin for middle age is *medium aevum*, and from this we get the word medieval). But of course men and women living then did not think of themselves as 'medieval people'! People's own lifetimes are, to them, the latest age. Remember that all such periods of history were invented long afterwards by scholars looking back at the past.

In this series of books the Middle Ages is taken to be roughly a thousand years, from the fifth century to the fifteenth. Some other books have slightly different divisions of time. But this is not important – the people, events and dates remain the same no matter which 'period' they are put in.

Note on the use of italics

Many teachers encourage pupils to build up their own glossaries of unfamiliar or foreign words and specialist or 'technical' terms relating to each historical period. To make this task easier, such words have been printed in *italics* at the point where they are explained in the text.

INTRODUCTION

THE COMING OF THE ENGLISH

> On Monday, May 8, I arrived at Sutton Hoo . . . upon my asking Mrs Pretty which mound she would like opened, she pointed to the largest of the group and said: 'What about this?' and I replied that it would be quite all right for me.

These words were written in 1939 by Mr Basil Brown, an *archaeologist* (a person who studies remains of the past) from Ipswich Museum. Little did he know that this brief conversation was to lead to the discovery of one of the richest treasures ever dug from British soil.

Mrs Edith Pretty was a Suffolk landowner. She had invited archaeologists to come and dig in the grounds of her estate, at Sutton Hoo, near Woodbridge. On sandy heathland alongside the estuary of the River Deben there was a group of *barrows* (earth mounds, which ancient peoples piled over the graves of the dead). Such burial mounds are quite common in Britain, but Mrs Pretty thought the ones on her estate might contain something out of the ordinary.

Treasure at Sutton Hoo

Three of the smaller barrows had been opened by Mr Brown on a previous visit in 1938. One contained traces of a small wooden boat, but robbers had broken into the mound and little else was left. Another mound held remains of two cremated bodies and a few objects of glass, bronze and stone. These early finds were a little disappointing. However, Mrs Pretty was determined not to give up, at least until the highest of the barrows had been opened. Mr Brown began this task in May 1939.

The position of Sutton Hoo

*The Sutton Hoo ship imprint
uncovered, 1939*

'The first find was a loose ship-nail and then five others in position', he wrote. 'We were definitely at one end of a ship.' The timber had rotted away, but the iron nails could still be seen and the decayed planks left a dark smear in the sandy soil. When the earth was scraped out, the imprint of a large rowing galley was clearly revealed. It was about 25 metres long and there were places for thirty-eight oarsmen.

This was an exciting discovery. However, by June it seemed that there might be much more than just traces of a ship. Work was stopped and, early in July, a team of experts from the British Museum took control of the site. Already rumours of a treasure were beginning to spread, so a police guard had to be provided.

Before long a collapsed burial chamber was found in the centre of the ship. Gently removing the soil with paintbrushes, the archaeologists uncovered a priceless treasure which had lain there for about 1,300 years. There were rare and beautiful pieces of English jewellery; fragments of a six-stringed musical instrument; gold coins from Gaul (France); silver spoons and bowls from as far away as Egypt and the eastern Mediterranean lands; a coat of chain-mail, rusted into a solid mass; a helmet, shield and sword from Sweden, and many other precious objects.

Great care was needed in removing the finds, because most of them were in a delicate condition. This work was finished only a few days before the outbreak of the Second World War (3 September 1939). According to the law, everything belonged to Mrs Pretty, but she generously decided to give her treasure to the nation. It was taken to the British Museum in London, where it can still be seen today.

Meanwhile, historians began trying to explain these strange and wonderful discoveries. Without doubt the ship was buried by people known as the Anglo-Saxons – the original 'English'. Most experts think the burial was in honour of a royal person. The ancient custom of putting a dead king in a ship with his treasure beside him was later described in an Old English poem called *Beowulf*:

'They set down their beloved king amidships, close by the mast. A mass of treasure was brought aboard from distant parts. No ship, they say, was ever so well equipped with swords, weapons and armour.'

The barrow containing the treasure ship photographed before the 'dig' began

This helmet was reconstructed out of hundreds of crumbling fragments found in the burial chamber of the Sutton Hoo ship. It took six months of continuous work to piece it together

But there is an unsolved mystery about Sutton Hoo. The ship contained no trace of a human body. So it was probably a memorial rather than a grave. From the dates on the coins, many historians believe that the burial commemorated a powerful king of East Anglia called Redwald, who died in 625 or thereabouts.

The absence of a body, however, has led other historians to connect the burial with Ethelhere – a later king of East Anglia who died in a battle in northern England in 654. Many of the warriors that day were swept away by a river in flood. This might explain the empty tomb. Perhaps Ethelhere's subjects believed his spirit would return to the ship, so they buried the things they thought he would need on his voyage to the after-world.

The present-day countries of north-western Europe

Who were the English?

The Anglo-Saxons, or English, came from the continent of Europe and began settling in Britain about 200 years before the time of the Sutton Hoo burial. Until about AD 400, Britain had been part of the great Roman Empire, which covered most of the known world.

In the fifth century, a great movement of peoples known as *barbarians* invaded the western half of this great Empire. To us a barbarian is a brutal, uncivilised person. But the Romans called all foreigners barbarians, even though many of them were far from being savages.

The Romans in Britain had been threatened by barbarian attacks many times before they left the country in about 410. They had fought to keep out the fierce Picts from the North, the Scots (then living in Ireland) who attacked the west coasts, and raiders called Saxons from across the North Sea. But when the Roman legions were ordered back to fight in Italy the Britons had to defend themselves.

The Saxons and other seafaring peoples from the Continent saw their chance. At first they had come for plunder; carrying away corn, weapons and slaves. But after the Roman legions had gone, they turned from piracy to full-scale invasion. The fertile soil and mild climate of Britain must have been very inviting to these tribes from the bleak, windswept lands of northern Europe.

The Romans, and many earlier peoples, left written records of their history. But hardly any barbarians could read or write. So the threads of history are difficult to unravel in the few centuries after the fall of the Roman Empire. We call this period the 'Dark Ages' because so little is known about it. Historians have to work like detectives, piecing together a story from a few scattered clues. This explains why the Sutton Hoo burial was such an exciting discovery.

The English invaders are usually said to have come from three different barbarian tribes – Angles, Saxons and Jutes. The Angles and Saxons probably came from the borderlands of present-day Denmark and West Germany (see map). But historians are still not sure about the Jutes. It used to be thought that their home-

North-western Europe in the fifth century: the homelands of the English invaders

land was in the part of Denmark we call Jutland (Jute-land). But archaeologists have found remains in the lands round the mouth of the River Rhine similar to those in the Jutish parts of England. Possibly Jutland was the original home of the Jutes before they moved south, first to the Rhine estuary and then, later, to England.

One thing we are sure about is a link between the language of the English settlers and that spoken by the Frisians, who lived in the area which is now the Netherlands. This may mean that there had been some mixing of the tribes in Frisia before the invasions began. No doubt Frisians took part in the great movement of peoples, just as Angles, Saxons and Jutes did. The Frisians had a good reason for wanting to leave home. Their lands, mostly at or below sea-level, were often flooded, and they had to build homes on artificial mounds to raise them above the surrounding marshland.

The story of Hengest and Horsa

There are no written eyewitness accounts dating from the start of the English invasions, so we have to rely upon stories passed on and written down many years later by monks. Much of our information comes from the Venerable Bede, a monk who wrote a detailed history of England 300 years after the Romans left Britain (see Chap. 3).

Although it was the Angles who later gave their name to England (Angleland) there is no evidence that they took a lead in the invasions. The first invaders to settle were said to have been a band of Jutes led by two brothers, Hengest and Horsa, in the year 449.

The story goes that a local British king called Vortigern had invited Hengest and Horsa to come and help him fight the northern Picts. In return, the Jutes were given the Isle of Thanet (which was not joined to the mainland, as it is today). But after sending for reinforcements from their homeland, the brothers turned against Vortigern. Horsa was killed, but Hengest overthrew the British leader and set up a kingdom of his own in Kent.

From then on a steady stream of settlers rowed across the sea to Britain. They sailed along the coasts and up the river estuaries – especially the Thames, Wash and Humber. The English invaders were primitive people who lived by hunting and farming. They were also warlike. After beaching their longboats, they marched inland, killing, plundering and burning as they went, taking the best land from the Britons (whom they called *Welsh* – their word for foreigners).

The boats which carried these settlers were rowing galleys. They held about sixty to eighty people, thirty of them at the oars. We know this from various remains that have been found. The best example was discovered in the last century, preserved in a peat bog at Nydam, near the Danish-German border. The 'Nydam ship', built of oak planks, dates from about 400. Such ships must have been very unsafe because the sides were only just above the waterline. Shipwrecks would have been common in storms and rough seas.

Experts say that an open voyage straight across the North Sea would have been madness in a ship like this; especially as there were no navigation charts or compasses. So the invaders almost

The Nydam ship. It is similar to the Sutton Hoo ship, but a few feet shorter and more simply built

certainly 'hugged the coastline' for most of the way. Perhaps they aimed to get to Cap Gris Nez, in France, where Channel swimmers start or finish? From here the English coast is just over twenty miles away and can be seen on a clear day.

A British revival – the legend of Arthur

Many Britons fled to escape the invaders. They went westwards, into the hills of what are now Cornwall and Devon, Wales, the Lake District and south-west Scotland. Some even crossed the seas, to Ireland or to Brittany in France. It must have been heartbreaking for them to leave their homes and crops, but even this was better than death or slavery.

However in some areas the Britons banded together and fought the invaders. Roughly 50 years after the first English settlements there seems to have been a British recovery. We learn from several sources that in about the year 500 the Britons won a big battle at a place called Mount Badon. They drove out the invaders from a large part of England and seem to have stopped their advance for more than half a century.

Written records suggest that the Britons had two successful war leaders at this time. The first, Ambrosius Aurelianus, was descended from a Roman family. After him, so we are told, came Arthur, the inspiration of many legends in later centuries. The earliest known reference to Arthur was made by a Welsh monk called Nennius, whose *History of the Britons* was probably written in the early ninth century. According to Nennius, Arthur – who was not himself a king – commanded the Britons in twelve major battles, of which only the last is given a name familiar to historians:

In that time the Saxons increased in numbers and their

This Iron Age hill fort at Badbury Rings in Dorset is thought by many historians to be the site of the battle of Mount Badon, where the Britons defeated the invaders.

strength grew in Britain . . . Then Arthur fought against those people in those days with the Kings of the Britons, but he himself was the . . . General in these battles . . . .

The twelfth battle was on Mount Badon where in one day nine hundred and sixty men fell in one charge of Arthur's. And no one laid them low but himself alone.

And in all these battles he stood out as victor.

It seems likely that Arthur was a real historical figure. But he would not have been much like the character in the famous stories of the Round Table. And his followers would not have been splendid knights like Sir Lancelot and Sir Galahad, although they may have fought on horseback. They would have been a band of brave Britons, fighting desperately to save their country from invasion.

The early English kingdoms

The Britons fought the invaders courageously, but in the end they failed. In the second half of the sixth century it seems that the Anglo-Saxons advanced inland and gained control of most of what is now England, together with parts of southern Scotland. The invaders were not used to living in towns, so the cities of Roman Britain declined in use and importance. Houses, baths, temples and other fine buildings crumbled and gradually weeds covered

The early English kingdoms, in about AD 600

the Roman roads. Even the Roman villas in the countryside were abandoned. The English settlers preferred to build their own rough timber huts, clustered together in villages surrounded by farm lands.

Powerful chieftains who had led the invaders in battle now became local kings. In time, the stronger kings conquered their weaker neighbours, so the number of kingdoms grew less. By the year 600 there were roughly a dozen of them. But during the next 100 years or so three kingdoms emerged as the most powerful: Northumbria, Mercia and Wessex (see map). At first Northumbria (which simply means 'north of the Humber') was the biggest. It grew out of the two smaller kingdoms of Bernicia and Deira. These were united by Ethelfrith, a strong king of Bernicia, who ruled from about 593 to 616.

It took many centuries for all the British strongholds in the western hills to be conquered. But over the rest of the country – England – few traces of the Britons or their customs were left. The English we now speak contains only a handful of *Celtic* (British) words. Most of these are the names of natural features in the countryside, such as the Chiltern and Mendip Hills, and the rivers Esk, Exe, Usk and Ouse. Names of towns and villages are mostly Anglo-Saxon, with endings such as -ing, -ton, -ham, -hay, -stead, -ley, -ly or -leigh, -field, -ford, -pool, -water and -mouth. This shows how complete the conquest of England was.

Timescale

AD
400   Romans leave Britain

450   Hengest and Horsa   ENGLISH INVASIONS
                                        ↓
500   Battle of Mount Badon   BRITISH REVIVAL
                                        ⋮
550   ↓
                                 ENGLISH
600   TRIUMPHANT
      Ethelfrith unites Northumbria

650   Sutton Hoo burial   ↓

Sources and questions

1. Look at the picture of the helmet on page 13.
   (a) The hero of the Old English poem, *Beowulf*, was presented with a helmet described as follows:

   At the crown of the helmet, the head-protector,
   Was a rim, with wire wound round it . . .

   How are these two pieces of evidence (the helmet and the extract from the poem) linked together?

(b) What do you think was the point of the projecting rim? How might it have given the wearer extra protection?

(c) Was the helmet designed to give extra protection to any other parts of the head?

(d) Compare this helmet with that of the Black Prince pictured on page 206. Which would you have preferred to wear in battle, and why?

2. Imagine it is AD 500 and your family has decided to sail to Britain from the land of the Saxons. Describe the voyage and landing. (Your story should be original, but based on the historical evidence.)

3. The following extract is taken from the *History of the English Church and People*, written in the early eighth century by the Venerable Bede.

> When the victorious invaders had scattered and destroyed the native peoples, . . . the Britons slowly began to take heart and recover their strength, emerging from the dens where they had hidden themselves, and joining in prayer that God might help them to avoid complete extermination. Their leader at this time was Ambrosius Aurelianus, a man of good character and the sole survivor of Roman race from the catastrophe. Under . . . his leadership the Britons took up arms, challenged their conquerors to battle, and with God's help inflicted a defeat on them. Thenceforward victory swung first to one side and then to the other, until the battle of Badon Hill, when the Britons made a considerable slaughter of the invaders.
>
> *Penguin Classics, 1955 (translated by Leo Sherley-Price), pages 57–8*

(a) What sorts of places do you think would have provided 'dens' for the Britons to hide in?

(b) Unlike the quotation from Nennius on pages 17–18, Bede does not mention Arthur. Are there any other points of disagreement between the two accounts?

(c) Pick out statements where you think Bede and Nennius may have been exaggerating.

(d) Which account do you think is likely to be nearer the truth? Give your reasons.

4. Many English place-names have the common Anglo-Saxon endings *-ton* (a farmstead or village), *-ham* (homestead, village) and *-ing* (place of a family or tribe).

(a) List the *ten* towns or villages nearest your home which have one of these endings.

(b) On a blank outline map of England, make a dot-map showing the overall distribution of *any one* of these place-name endings. Does your map tell you anything about the nature of the English settlements?

MONKS AND MISSIONARIES

THE ROMAN CHURCH – ST BENEDICT AND GREGORY 'THE GREAT'

About the year 500 a young man named Benedict left his comfortable home in central Italy and travelled to Rome. His parents, who were wealthy Christians, had sent him to finish his education and prepare to work in government service.

The Rome that greeted Benedict was very different from the proud city that for centuries had ruled the Mediterranean world. During the previous 100 years 'barbarian' invaders from the north had ransacked the city. They had destroyed public buildings, carrying away tonnes of valuables, melted down beautiful bronze statues, smashed stone monuments and left the streets littered with rubble. Even the great *aqueducts* (canals on bridges) which fed the city's taps and fountains were broken down or choked with vegetation.

Many people had left the city and there were open spaces where houses once stood. The palace of the emperors was deserted. The most important citizen was now the Bishop of Rome – the *Pope* (father) of the Christian Church. Christianity had become the official religion of the Roman Empire and there were by this time many Christians in western Europe, including barbarians who had been converted. Some of them still looked to Rome and the Pope for leadership and guidance.

St Benedict, as depicted in a later medieval manuscript

St Benedict

Benedict was a deeply religious young man. He was shocked by the lawless and sinful behaviour of many Romans. So he gave up his studies, left the city and travelled eastwards to the hills. There, on the mountain of Subiaco, he found a cave and lived alone as

St Simeon Stylites, as shown in a modern film of his life

a hermit. To Benedict it seemed the best way of getting closer to God and living a truly Christian life.

This was not a new idea. Long before Benedict was born, men in Egypt and other eastern Mediterranean lands had gone into the deserts to escape the wickedness of the world and be alone with their God. Such men were called *monks*. The word really means 'one who lives alone', but often monks gathered in communities, working and praying together. This way of life soon spread to parts of the West, including Ireland.

The earliest monks believed it did them good to suffer hardship. They cut out 'luxuries' like soft beds and comfortable clothes. They fasted for long periods and spent night after night praying instead of sleeping. Some went to extremes, whipping themselves or rolling naked among thorns. In the Syrian desert, St Simeon Stylites worshipped God from a platform on top of a tall pillar. There was no room to lie down and no protection from the blazing sun. To get food and drink Simeon lowered a basket on the end of a rope. Yet he stayed up there for thirty-three years. St Daniel, one of his followers, later beat his 'record' by three months.

Such achievements did not interest Benedict. Once, when he saw a hermit chained to a rock, he said: 'If you are God's servant, let the chain of Christ not any iron chain hold thee.' Benedict wore animal skins, ate dry bread and lived a quiet, simple life. Before long, religious men in Rome heard about the monk in the hills and went to visit him. Some asked if they could stay. So Benedict organised a community of monks who all agreed to give up worldly pleasures and pray to God.

After some years Benedict left Subiaco with a small band of his closest followers. They travelled south, to the top of a hill overlooking the village of Monte Cassino, and there, about the year 525, Benedict founded his first and most famous monastery. He lived at Monte Cassino until his death in 543. Some of the time he spent writing a *Rule* for monks to live by. This 'Benedictine Rule', which is in fact a large number of rules, is still practised today by monks in many countries.

The monastery at Monte Cassino had grown to look like this by the early twentieth century. It was the centre of a great battle in the Second World War, after which a fine new monastery was built on the site of the old

The Benedictine 'Rule'

St Benedict's idea of a monastery was a place where ordinary men would want to come and lead a Christian life, praying and working together. He ordered that the monks' clothes, although plain, should be warm and comfortable. They were to have a good eight hours of sleep, and two daily meals of simple but nourishing food.

Nevertheless it was far from an easy life in a Benedictine monastery. The abbot, elected by the monks, or brothers, to rule the community, had to be obeyed at all times, without the slightest question or delay. Through regular obedience, a monk would always be humble and never get a high opinion of himself. As Benedict put it in his *Rule*:

> Everywhere, sitting or walking or standing, let him always be
> with head inclined, his looks fixed upon the ground;
> remembering every hour that he is guilty of his sins.

No personal belongings were allowed. Even a monk's clothes were the property of the monastery. A monk could not receive a letter from his parents without the abbot's agreement. On top of this there were strict rules about silence. The monks were rarely allowed to speak to each other. And, of course, all relationships with women were forbidden.

Only a truly devoted Christian would be able to keep such difficult rules. So Benedict ordered that each newcomer, or *novice*, would have a year 'on probation' before having to make his solemn promises of obedience to the Rule. But once he had promised, he was expected to belong to the monastery all his life. He could not step outside the walls without the abbot's permission. 'He must know', wrote Benedict, 'that he has henceforth no power even over his own body.'

The daily life of the community began before dawn, and every part of it was timetabled. At regular intervals all the brothers gathered in their chapel to pray and sing God's praises. There were eight separate services each day, which took about five hours altogether. The rest of the time was fully occupied, for, as Benedict said:

> Idleness is the enemy of the soul. And therefore, at fixed times,
> the brothers ought to be occupied in manual labour; and at
> other fixed hours, in holy reading.

So every day, except Sunday, about seven hours were spent doing ordinary work such as farming, cooking, cleaning, caring for the sick, writing and copying books, or teaching boys and younger monks.

St Benedict's *Rule* was practical and full of common sense. In the years to come monasteries all over Europe copied it. Nuns, too, lived according to its basic vows of *obedience*, *poverty* (no belongings) and *chastity* (no sexual relationships). Later, some 'double houses' were founded, where both monks and nuns lived under the rule of an abbess. The men and women were carefully

Position of Benedict's
monasteries

Modern Benedictine monks
doing their own building. All
work is done for God and is
considered to be a form of
prayer

kept apart. At one double house in England the abbess would only
speak to the monks through a window!

In those troubled times Benedictine monasteries were among
the few places where people could find peace, order and good
living. Their example encouraged ordinary Christians to live
better lives. Monasteries were also centres of learning and
education. Monks taught the young, kept historical records and
made copies of the Scriptures and many other books. Without
their efforts most of the writings of the ancient world would have
been unknown in the barbarian kingdoms of the West.

Gregory 'the Great'

In Benedict's lifetime the *Rule* was only followed in monasteries
he set up himself. It later became famous mainly through the
efforts of a pope – Gregory I, called 'the Great'.

Like Benedict, Gregory was born into a wealthy family, about
the year 540. His father had a large house in Rome and could
afford to give his son a good education. Gregory soon showed
outstanding ability. He was only in his early thirties when he was
chosen *Prefect* of Rome, the highest position in the government
of the city.

Pope Gregory gives his blessing to some of the poor and unfortunate people of Rome

It was a time of great hardship for the people. Italy was again being invaded by barbarians – the fierce Lombards ('Longbeards') who came from north Germany. Pouring through the Alps, they quickly overran most of northern Italy (part of this area is still called Lombardy today). Seeing all the misery and destruction around him, Gregory felt sure the world was coming to an end. He wrote:

> Beaten down by so many blows, the ancient kingdom [Rome] has fallen from its glory and shows us now another kingdom [Heaven], which is coming, which is already near.

After only a year as *Prefect*, Gregory decided to give up his position and devote his life to serving God. His father had just died, leaving a large fortune. Gregory gave some to charity and used the rest to set up six monasteries in Sicily. His own house in Rome was turned into a seventh, and there Gregory became a monk.

Not long afterwards some monks from Monte Cassino arrived in Rome. They had gone there to escape the attacks of the Lombards. We cannot be certain, but it was probably from these monks that Gregory first learned about the *Rule* of St Benedict. It was a great inspiration to him and he put it into practice in his own monastery. Later he wrote about Benedict's life and work, making it known to Christians in many countries.

'The first of the great popes'

The most important part of Gregory's life began in 590, a year of floods and plague, when he was chosen to be Pope. By then he was in poor health. Yet right up to his death, in 604, he worked tirelessly to strengthen the organisation of the Church and to unite Christians in many lands. He kept in close contact with bishops and clergy, and wrote a special handbook called *The Pastoral Rule*, which told them how to carry out their duties.

Above all, Gregory worked to spread the faith among *heathens* (those who were not Christians). The barbarian king of Spain was converted by missionaries sent by Gregory, and most of the King's subjects soon became Christians. Gregory also sent a band of monks to convert the English. The outcome of this important mission is described in the next chapter.

The Church was only part of Gregory's concern. He also felt responsible for the poor and plague-stricken people of Rome. Whenever he heard that a beggar had died of hunger he blamed himself for it. As Pope, Gregory received the income from a number of large estates. He used most of it to provide free food, clothing and medical care for the needy. He even organised the defence of Rome against the Lombards, and finally made a peace treaty with them.

Nothing seemed too difficult for Gregory, or too small to escape his attention. The vast amount of work he got through can be seen from the hundreds of letters he wrote, which are still preserved. They were addressed not only to Church leaders and missionaries, but also to kings, queens and tribal chiefs. In a time of invasion, plague and famine, the organisation of the Roman Church might easily have collapsed, just like the Roman Empire, had it not been for Gregory's work. He has been rightly called 'the first of the great popes'.

Gregory the Great (hands upraised) leads a procession to pray for the end of a dreadful plague in Rome (590)

Sources and questions

1. Look at the picture on page 25.
    (a) How does the Pope's clothing set him apart from the other men?
    (b) The artist has shown a devil coming out of one man's mouth. What do you think is happening to this man?
    (c) Why do you think the same man has his hands tied and is being held by the man on the right?
    (d) Why is the man on the left, nearest the Pope, holding a bowl?
    (e) Can you work out what the man with the bundle of twigs in his hand is doing?

2. Draw up a list of instructions you imagine Pope Gregory may have given the missionaries he sent to convert the

heathens in Spain and England. What dangers and difficulties might he have warned them of?

3. The following extract is taken from St Benedict's *Rule*.

> We are about to start a school for the service of God in which we hope nothing harsh or burdensome will be demanded. . . . Prompt obedience is required of all monks. They live not as they themselves would choose, but . . . agree to be ruled by the abbot. . . . If it be possible let them all sleep in a common dormitory. . . . The younger brothers are not to have their beds next to each other, but amongst those of the elders. When they rise for the service of God let them gently encourage one another, because of the excuses made by those who are drowsy. . . . No one, without the abbot's permission, shall give, receive or keep as his own anything whatever: neither book nor writing-tablet nor pen. . . . Monks shall practise silence at all times, but especially at night-time. So, on coming out from Compline (the last service of the day), no one shall be allowed to speak at all. . . . Monks must not grumble about the colour or rough material of their clothes. . . . A mattress, blanket, coverlet and pillow are enough for bedding. The beds shall be frequently searched by the abbot to guard against the vice of hoarding. . . . A monastery ought to be so arranged that everything necessary – that is, water, a mill, a garden, a bakery – may be made use of . . . so that there shall be no need for the monks to wander about outside. For this is not at all good for their souls.

(a) By the standards of his day, Benedict's rules were not 'harsh or burdensome'. But we might think differently now. Which would you find the hardest of these rules to live by, and why?

(b) How are these rules linked to the monks' vows of (i) poverty and (ii) obedience?

(c) Is there any rule in the above extract which might have helped monks to keep their vow of chastity?

(d) Give *three* examples from the extract of ways in which Benedict takes into account ordinary human failings.

4. In the Second World War there was a great battle at Monte Cassino. Find out who fought in the battle and what happened to the monastery.

HEATHENS BECOME CHRISTIANS

Christianity first came to Britain when the country was part of the Roman Empire. But the English invaders were heathens, so Christian worship died out wherever they settled. The English wore charms to keep away evil spirits, and they believed giants, dragons and other monsters lived in the lonely moors, woods and swamps. They worshipped nature gods and made sacrifices to them.

Chief among their gods was *Woden*. Nearly all Anglo-Saxon kings claimed to be descended from him. Other gods included *Tiw*, a war-god; *Thunor*, god of thunder, the sound of which was believed to come from his chariot rolling across the heavens; and *Frig*, a goddess supposed to bring good harvests. All are still remembered in our days of the week – Tuesday (Tiw), Wednesday (Woden), Thursday (Thunor) and Friday (Frig). Saturday probably comes from *Saturn*, the Roman god of agriculture. Sunday and Monday are named after the sun and moon, both worshipped by the Anglo-Saxons.

The heathen English certainly expected some kind of future life. Otherwise they would not have buried the goods of the dead – as at Sutton Hoo. But we cannot be sure what kind of afterworld they believed in.

Augustine's mission

The Venerable Bede tells us that some years before Gregory the Great became Pope, he was struck by the sight of some fair-haired, light-skinned boys being sold as slaves in a Roman market place. He learned that they were Angles from Northumbria. It shocked him to think that such fine young men were ignorant of Christianity.

When he became Pope, Gregory decided to send missionaries to convert the English. He gathered a party of forty monks from his own monastery in Rome. Under their leader, Augustine, they landed on the Isle of Thanet in Kent, in 597. The king of Kent, Ethelbert, had a Christian wife called Bertha. She was a princess from the kingdom of the Franks (now France) which had been converted 100 years before. Ethelbert himself was still a heathen.

Bronze figure of an Anglo-Saxon god

St Augustine – from a fifteenth-century Italian painting

The Church of St Martin at Canterbury, used by Augustine's mission. It still has a few Roman bricks in its walls today

But he agreed to meet Augustine, so long as it was in the open air, where he believed his visitors would be unable to work their magic on him!

Ethelbert must have been surprised by the sight of shaven-headed monks, wearing black Benedictine robes and chanting in a strange language. But he decided to trust them. He gave them food and shelter in Canterbury and allowed them to preach to his people. With Queen Bertha's permission, the monks used the old Roman church of St Martin – one of the few not destroyed in the invasions.

This small medallion was found in St Martin's churchyard in Canterbury. It bears the words 'LEUDARDUS EPS' (EPS is short for Episcopi, the Latin for bishop). It therefore seems to confirm the accuracy of the following passage in Bede's History: '[Ethelbert had] . . . a Christian wife of the Frankish royal house named Bertha, whom he had received from her parents on condition that she should have freedom to hold and practise her faith unhindered with Bishop Liudhard, whom they had sent as her helper in the faith.'

Before the year was out Ethelbert had been baptised a Christian, and so had thousands of his people. Soon more converts were gained in the neighbouring kingdoms. It was an encouraging start. Gregory made Augustine Archbishop of Canterbury and sent him instructions on how to organise the English Church. He advised Augustine not to destroy the heathen temples but to change them into churches, replacing the idols with altars. Gregory also suggested turning the heathen sacrifices into the regular Christian festivals. Christmas therefore replaced the winter feast of Yule, and Easter is still named after a Saxon spring goddess, *Eostre*.

The Roman mission finally took root in England, but not before it had suffered a series of setbacks. Both Gregory and Augustine died in 604. Soon afterwards there was a return to heathen ways in many parts of south-eastern England. In East Anglia, King Redwald decided to have the best of both worlds. He kept two altars in the same temple: one for Christ and one for the heathen gods!

The only bright spot was the conversion of Edwin, king of Northumbria. He married a Christian daughter of Ethelbert in 625, and within two years her chaplain had baptised the King and many of his subjects. But then disaster struck the kingdom. In 632 Edwin was defeated and killed by the heathen king of Mercia. The Queen fled to Kent with her children, while many of the people returned to their old heathen ways. The northern English were soon brought back to Christianity, but not by the Roman missionaries.

Christians from Ireland

Right through the years of Anglo-Saxon settlement, the Christian faith had been kept alive in the unconquered western parts of Britain. Ireland in particular became a stronghold of Christianity through the efforts of St Patrick, a Briton who became a monk in Gaul. In the middle of the fifth century Patrick travelled throughout Ireland preaching and baptising the people. After about thirty years he and his followers had made Ireland a Christian country.

A century later, in 563, an Irish monk named Columba sailed across to the land of the heathen Picts (see map on page 34). On the tiny island of Iona he and twelve other monks set up a monastery. First they cleared the land and planted crops. Then they began to convert the Picts on the mainland. When Columba died (in 597 – the year Augustine landed in Kent) the English were the only people in the British Isles who had not heard the teachings of Christ.

Iona remained an important centre of the British, or *Celtic*, Church. It was from there that Christianity came back to northern England after the death of King Edwin in 632. The next Northumbrian king, Oswald, had been Edwin's rival. He had been forced to leave Northumbria and spent many years in exile on Iona. There he learned Christian teachings from Columba's followers. Naturally when he became king he turned to Iona for help in restoring the faith among his people. A small company of Irish monks arrived in 635, under their leader Aidan. They chose to build their monastery on the island of Lindisfarne. This is just off the coast, although at low tide it is possible to walk across the sands to the mainland.

Aidan and his companions walked all over the hills and dales of northern England, preaching, setting up monasteries and

The abbey of Iona today, with the island of Mull in the background

training monks. Some of them later travelled south to preach to the peoples of Mercia, East Anglia and Essex. Although King Oswald was killed in battle (642) the work of Aidan and his monks went on, encouraged by the new king, Oswy. Lindisfarne became so famous as a place of God that it was called 'Holy Island'.

The synod at Whitby

Christianity, therefore, came to the English by two different routes. Roman missionaries converted many people in the South, bringing them into the Roman *Catholic* (or universal) Church. The conversion of the North and Midlands was led by 'Celtic' Christians from Iona.

For more than 200 years these Celts had been cut off from the rest of the Christian world. Consequently they had developed customs and practices of their own. They had a different baptism service, celebrated Easter at an earlier date than other Christians and did not follow the Pope's leadership. Celtic monks even had a different *tonsure* (haircut). Instead of shaving the crown of the head, which was usual, they shaved a semicircular patch from ear to ear.

All these differences caused much confusion. In the Northumbrian court King Oswy followed Celtic practices, while his queen (Edwin's daughter who escaped to Kent) had been taught the Roman ways. So Easter was celebrated twice in the same household.

Oswy wanted to bring all English Christians together. In 663 he called a *synod*, or council, of the Northumbrian Church at Whitby. Christian leaders from all over the country were invited. The main business of the meeting was to agree on the dating of Easter. But behind this lay a much bigger question. Were the Celtic Christians willing to accept the leadership of the Roman Church?

In the end the arguments of the Roman Christians (see document 4 on page 39) convinced Oswy. All present agreed with the King, except a few Celtic monks who went back to Iona. From now on English bishops were in touch with Rome and other parts of Europe. Gradually, during the next century, Celtic Christians in Scotland, Ireland and Wales came to accept Roman customs.

The different tonsures of Celtic and Roman monks. Which is which?

Theodore and Boniface

Soon after the meeting at Whitby, the Pope had to appoint a new Archbishop of Canterbury. He chose a wise Greek monk named Theodore, who was then living in Rome. Theodore arrived in England in 669 and continued the task of uniting Celtic and Roman Christians in one Church. He held regular councils of bishops from both sides to help sort out the many differences that remained.

The Celtic Church was based on monasteries. But the Roman Church was organised differently. Countries were divided into large districts called *dioceses*, each under a bishop with a cathedral church. In later centuries dioceses were sub-divided into *parishes*, each with a priest to serve the religious needs of the people. Theodore increased the number of dioceses and appointed many new bishops. He also saw that schools were set up for training priests. This was a very long task. Even 300 years later there were still some villages without a regular priest or church.

Church building was costly. Most people had to do without a parish church until perhaps a wealthy lord built one. In the meantime monks or priests set up large crosses in the open air, and villagers gathered round them for services. Some of these 'wayside crosses' were made of rough wood. Others were built of stone and delicately carved.

One of the finest stone crosses can still be seen at Ruthwell, near Dumfries. It is six metres high and has beautiful carvings on it, some showing scenes from the life of Jesus. Down the sides there is part of an Old English poem, *The Dream of the Rood*. The rood is the cross of Christ, and the poem tells how the rood felt when Jesus hung upon it:

I trembled in his clasp, yet dared not bow nor fall to earth. . .
They pierced me with dark nails, you see the wounds . . .
stained was I with the blood that streamed.

The Ruthwell Cross. It is now inside the village church

Escomb Church in County Durham. Built in the seventh or eighth century, it is still almost complete today

Even before the last heathens had been converted at home, English monks began preaching on the Continent – in the homelands of their ancestors. In 690, the year of Theodore's death, a Northumbrian monk named Willibrord sailed to Frisia with a dozen companions. For almost fifty years he worked to convert the people, and founded several monasteries and churches. The Pope made Willibrord bishop over the part of Frisia he had brought into the Church.

The greatest of all Anglo-Saxon missionaries was Boniface, a monk from Wessex. In 718 he left England, never to return. Travelling deep into the heart of heathen Germany, he personally converted thousands of people in the lands east of the Rhine. His progress was closely followed in Rome, and also by his friends in England. Boniface became an archbishop and set about organising the first Christian Church in Germany. Englishmen who went out to help him became abbots of new monasteries, priests and even bishops.

Boniface was never at rest. When he was well over seventy he left Germany to work among the Frisians (many were still heathens). But there the 'Apostle of Germany' met his death. Just after dawn on 5 June 754, Boniface was about to confirm some new converts when a band of unbelievers appeared and brutally murdered him.

Bede – scholar of Northumbria

Most of our knowledge of the English conversions comes from the *History of the English Church and People*, completed in 731 by the monk Bede. Indeed, we depend on this book for much of what we know about English history in general in the previous 300 years.

Bede grew up in Northumbria at the time of Archbishop Theodore. It was an unusual childhood, because when he was seven his parents entrusted him to the care of monks at Wearmouth – a fine new Benedictine monastery. The abbot, Benedict Biscop, spent many years studying and travelling in Italy and France. He brought stonemasons from the Continent to build Wearmouth – and also a second monastery he founded nearby at Jarrow. More important for the future of Bede, Biscop returned from visits to Rome with large quantities of books. His monasteries soon had libraries as good as any in England.

Bede left Wearmouth when he was still a boy and spent the rest of his life at Jarrow. It took him many years to collect all the information for his *History*. He carefully studied old Anglo-Saxon stories, songs and poems. Monks from all over the country sent documents, and some came to talk to him. A priest from London even visited Rome for Bede, to look at Pope Gregory's letters to Augustine. The finished book, written in Latin, was very detailed yet clear and easy to read.

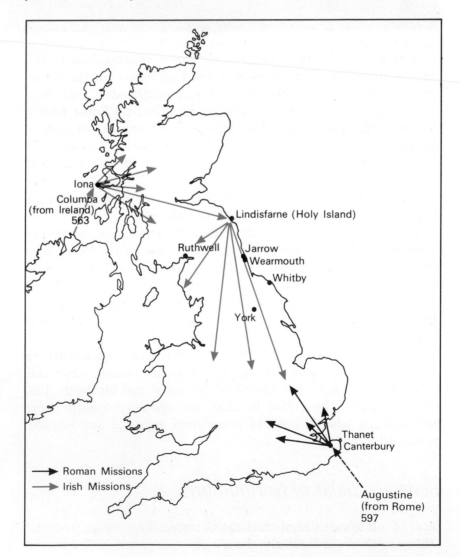

The conversion of the English, from north and south

A manuscript illustration of the Venerable Bede

Bede's *History* was almost the last of a long series of books, which earned him the name 'Venerable' (worthy of respect). Most were explanations of the Scriptures, or textbooks for pupils in the monastery school. Bede thought of himself mainly as a teacher. At a time when there were no ordinary schools, education was chiefly carried on in monasteries. Nearly all books were in Latin, the language of the Scriptures and church services.

In 735, the year of Bede's death, York became the home of a second archbishop. From then on York cathedral school was the main centre of learning in Northumbria. Its library was one of the best in western Europe. Alcuin, master of the school for fifteen years, later went to the court of Charlemagne, king of the Franks. He did much to spread Northumbrian standards of education on the Continent.

There were educated people in all parts of England – not just Northumbria – as we know from the southerners who helped Bede or wrote to Boniface in Germany. Archbishop Theodore set up an excellent cathedral school at Canterbury which taught Greek as well as Latin. So the Christian conversions helped to civilise the once barbarous English. By the time of Bede and Alcuin they had become well known for their faith and learning.

Timeline   The English Conversions

AD

432–61	Mission of St Patrick to the Irish
563	St Columba sails to Iona
597	Arrival of Augustine's Mission from Rome
635	St Aidan goes to Lindisfarne
663	Synod at Whitby
669–90	Theodore Archbishop of Canterbury
718–54	Boniface's Mission to the Germans
735	Death of Venerable Bede

Irish missionaries taught Northumbrian monks the art of beautiful writing and book decoration with coloured inks. This is a decorated page from a famous copy of the four Gospels made at Lindisfarne, about AD 700. The 'Lindisfarne Gospels', which are kept in the British Museum, have gold, silver and jewels set in the cover

DOCUMENTS: THE ROMAN CHURCH TAKES ROOT

Document 1

Here is part of a letter written in 601 by Pope Gregory to the newly converted King Ethelbert. It is reproduced in Bede's *History of the English Church and People*.

> To our excellent son, the most glorious King Ethelbert, King of the English. . . .
>
> The reason why Almighty God raises good men to govern nations is that through them He may bestow the gifts of His mercy on all whom they rule. We know that this is so in the case of the English nation, over whom you reign so gloriously. . . . Therefore, my illustrious son, . . . press on with the task of extending the Christian Faith among the people under your charge. Make their conversion your first concern; stop the worship of idols, and destroy their shrines; raise the moral standards of your subjects by your own innocence of life, encouraging, warning, persuading, correcting, and showing them an example by your good deeds.

Adapted from A History of the English Church and People, *Penguin Classics, 1955, page 89*

Questions

1. What do you think was Gregory's purpose in writing this letter?
2. In what sense does Gregory refer to Ethelbert as a 'son'?
3. Does the title Gregory gives the King flatter him? (If you are not sure, look at the map of the early English kingdoms on page 18). Does Gregory try to flatter Ethelbert in any other way?
4. What does Gregory think is Ethelbert's most important task as a Christian King?
5. Why does Gregory consider the King's personal conduct to be so important?

On the right-hand side of this whalebone casket, made in Northumbria in the seventh century, we see the three wise kings bearing their gifts. What do you think the flower-like object above them is meant to represent? What other details can you pick out?

Document 2

Gregory the Great's *Pastoral Rule* was completed in 591, just after he became Pope. Augustine would almost certainly have brought a copy with him to England six years later. In this extract, Gregory offers advice to the clergy about preaching the word of God.

The teacher is to know that he is by no means to impose on any man more than he can bear, in case the rope of his mind be overstretched till it breaks. Therefore lofty doctrine is better concealed from many men, and preached to few. . . . St Paul said: '. . . since in your faith you are still children, I must still give you milk to drink, not meat to eat.' . . . So every wise teacher must preach open and clear doctrine to the dark minds, and not yet give out any secret and deep doctrine. But when he sees the dark minds of foolish men approaching somewhat to the light of truth, he must reveal to them more secret and deeper doctrine out of the holy books.

Edited for the Early English Text Society, 1871, by Henry Sweet, pages 458 and 460

Questions

1. Why do you think Gregory felt it necessary to offer this advice?
2. It is not usual nowadays to refer to a priest as a teacher. Why was it an especially suitable description in Gregory's day?
3. Give at least two examples of basic Christian beliefs or doctrines which in your opinion would be too 'lofty' for 'dark minds'.
4. Can you think of any possible pitfalls that might result from preaching in the way Gregory advises?

Document 3

The importance to Christians of the matters discussed at the Synod of Whitby is clear in this extract from a letter written about fifty years later by Ceolfrid, the abbot of Bede's monastery at Jarrow, to Nechtan, King of the Picts. (Bede almost certainly composed the letter on Ceolfrid's behalf.)

Having written about Easter as you requested, . . . I also urge you to make sure that the tonsure, about which you also asked me to write, is worn in accordance with the practice of the Christian Church. . . . We are not shaven in the form of a crown solely because Peter was shorn in this way, but because Peter was shorn in this way in memory of our Lord's Passion. . . . Those who have taken monastic vows or are in Holy Orders should discipline themselves more strictly for our Lord's sake, and wear their heads tonsured in the form of the crown of thorns which Christ wore on His head in His Passion. . . . In this way their own appearance will be a reminder to them to be willing and ready to suffer ridicule and disgrace for His sake.

Adapted from A History of the English Church and People, *Penguin Classics, 1955, pages 324–5*

Questions

1. Although there is no evidence that St Peter was tonsured in the Roman, or any other, style, why do you think Ceolfrid claims that he was?
2. What is meant by 'our Lord's Passion'? Why is the shape of the Roman tonsure a reminder of this?
3. What is the difference between taking monastic vows and being in Holy Orders?
4. Do you find the arguments in this letter convincing? Give reasons for your opinion.

Document 4

The Synod of Whitby (663) firmly established the practices of the Roman Church in England. Speaking for the Roman side at the synod was Wilfred, abbot of a monastery at Ripon, who had spent some years on the Continent. Bede tells us that he put his case as follows.

When Wilfred had received the King's command to speak, he said: 'Our Easter customs are . . . generally followed throughout . . . the world wherever the Church of Christ has spread. The only people who stupidly hold out against the whole world are these Scots and their obstinate supporters the Picts and Britons, who inhabit only a part of these the two outermost islands of the ocean. . . . And even if your Columba – or, may I say, ours also if he was the servant of Christ – was a saint able to perform miracles, can he take precedence before the most blessed Prince of the Apostles, to whom our Lord said: *"Thou art Peter, and upon this rock I will build my Church, and the gates of hell shall not prevail against it, and I will give thee the keys of the kingdom of heaven"*?' . . .

At this, the King concluded: 'Then, I tell you, Peter is guardian of the gates of heaven, and I shall not contradict him. I shall obey his commands in everything to the best of my knowledge and ability; otherwise, when I come to the gates of heaven, there may be no one to open them, because he who holds the keys has turned away.'

When the King said this, all present, both high and low, showed their agreement and, giving up their imperfect customs, hastened to adopt those which they had learned to be better.

Adapted from A History of the English Church and People, *Penguin Classics, 1955, pages 188–9, 192*

Questions

1. Summarise, each in a sentence, Wilfred's two main arguments in favour of adopting the Roman ways.
2. What does Wilfred mean when he refers to Britain and Ireland as 'the two outermost islands of the ocean'?
3. Why does Wilfred speak of 'your' Columba? To what extent had Columba's work made the Synod necessary?
4. Why did the King (Oswy) appear to be fearful of contradicting St Peter?
5. What evidence is there in this passage that Bede is biased towards the Roman side?

St Paul's Church, Jarrow. The wall in the foreground is part of the monastery as it was in the later Middle Ages. A small Saxon round-headed window can be seen beside the drainpipe on the right of the picture. Why do you think windows were so small in Anglo-Saxon times?

BYZANTINES, ARABS AND FRANKS

JUSTINIAN AND MOHAMMED

Justinian was one of the greatest Roman emperors. Yet he lived in the sixth century, after the fall of Rome, and his palace was nearly 1000 miles from that city! There is a simple explanation. In its later years the Roman Empire was divided into two halves, each with an emperor. The western half grew weak and was overrun by barbarians, in the fifth century. But the other half – the lands round the eastern Mediterranean – remained strong and prosperous.

It was this *East* Roman Empire that Justinian ruled, from 527 to 565. His capital was Constantinople, one of the world's richest and best defended cities (see map on page 42). It was surrounded by water on three sides, and several stout walls protected the land approach to the city from enemy invasion. Its great harbour, seven miles long, was crowded with ships from many lands.

In the Emperor's magnificent palace, decorated with gold, silver, richly coloured tapestries and mosaics, six regiments of guards protected his sacred person. Justinian considered himself responsible only to God. No one could ever accuse him of making a mistake. Anyone wanting to ask a favour would do so on their knees. Even so, it was said that Justinian never did anything without taking the advice of his wife – the intelligent and beautiful Empress Theodora. She was the daughter of a circus animal-trainer, and Justinian had to change the law before he could marry a woman of such humble birth.

The conquests of Justinian

As a boy, Justinian had learned about the past glories of Rome, in the days when its emperors ruled all the Mediterranean world.

His greatest ambition was to recover the western lands lost to the barbarians. He once wrote: 'We have taken hope that the Lord will grant us the rest of the Empire, which the Romans of old . . . lost through idleness.' Certainly Justinian was not idle. He worked such long hours that it was said in his court, 'the Emperor never sleeps'.

Justinian began his 'war of reconquest' by attacking the Vandals in North Africa – the weakest of the barbarian kingdoms. In 533 his finest general, Belisarius, set sail with 15,000 troops and landed not far from Carthage. Belisarius's foot-soldiers were fierce fighters, mostly recruited from tribes along the borders of the Empire. His cavalrymen, in their chain-mail coats and iron helmets, were the best in the world. The Vandal army was overrun and, within six months, a large part of North Africa was again a 'Roman' province.

Belisarius next attacked the East-Goths in Italy – Justinian's main goal. Approaching by way of Sicily, he soon captured Rome (537) and Ravenna (540). The war seemed to be won. But the enemy suddenly recovered and fighting dragged on until 553, when the Goths were finally defeated. Large parts of Italy suffered great damage. Rome, which was captured and re-captured several times, became almost a heap of wreckage.

Finally, Justinian's forces moved against the West-Goths in Spain. But after hard fighting they captured only the south-eastern corner of the kingdom. Much of the old Western Empire was still

Mosaic from the wall of the church of San Vitale, Ravenna, showing the Emperor Justinian with his attendants

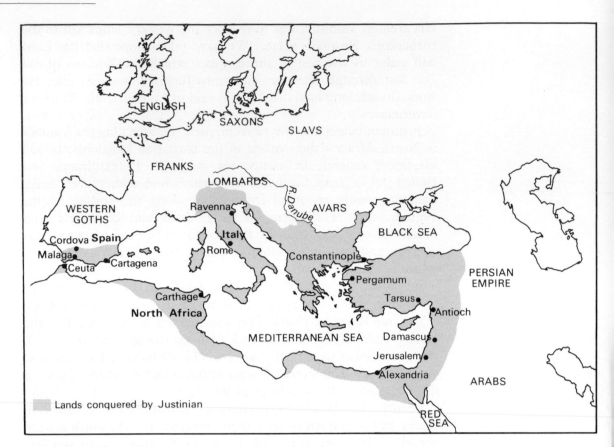

The Empire of Justinian,
at its fullest extent

in barbarian hands when Justinian died. However, the Emperor controlled the sea-routes, so at least the Mediterranean was again a 'Roman lake'.

The last emperor to speak Latin

Justinian's wars were very costly, in both money and lives. His subjects were forced to pay crippling taxes for the upkeep of the army. And all the time the Emperor needed extra forces to protect the heart of his empire from the powerful Persians and the peoples beyond the Danube frontier. In the end, his conquests were short-lived. Only a few years after his death most of Italy was overrun by the Lombards. Within a century the foothold in Spain was lost and North Africa was conquered by Arab tribesmen.

Nowadays Justinian is remembered more as a reformer of Roman law than as a conqueror. Over the centuries there had been so many changes in the law that magistrates often did not know what was the correct judgment. So Justinian ordered a team of experts to sort out all that was best in the old Roman laws. The result was the great four-part *Corpus Juris Civilis* (Body of Civil Law) which is still in use today. This vast work fills over 2,000 closely printed pages in a modern edition. It has influenced the laws of many present-day countries in Europe and the Americas.

Justinian is also famous for his buildings – especially the magnificent church of *Santa Sophia* (Holy Wisdom) in Constantinople, which still stands. It took 10,000 men five years to build.

The ceiling was overlaid with pure gold, and sunlight flooding through the huge domed roof lit up richly coloured marble floors and walls. A writer of the time said of *Santa Sophia:* 'Whenever one goes there to pray . . . one's heart is lifted up to God and finds itself in heaven.'

Emperors ruled at Constantinople for 900 years after Justinian. But none of them tried to re-conquer the West. They were kept busy defending the empire they already had. As contacts with western Europe grew less the old Roman customs disappeared. Before long even the Christianity of the Eastern Empire was different from that of the Roman Catholic Church. The Empire became known as *Byzantium* – the name of the ancient Greek city which once stood on the site of Constantinople. Certainly its way of life was Greek rather than Roman. In fact Justinian was the last emperor to speak Latin.

A Prophet from Arabia

Seventy years after Justinian's death Byzantium was attacked from an unexpected direction. Thousands of armed Bedouins from Arabia advanced upon its fertile lands. This was not the first time that Arabs had left their homeland in large numbers. Arabia is one of the driest countries in the world. Most of it is desert, scorching hot by day and bitterly cold by night. Most Arabs lived as nomads, moving from place to place in search of pasture for livestock. An increase in the Arab population could lead to food shortages and force tribesmen to search for richer grazing lands.

Church of Santa Sophia in Istanbul. The tall minarets and some extensions were added by the Turks many centuries later. But the main building dates back to the 530s

A camel caravan

Crowds gather round the sacred Kaaba *in the modern city of Mecca*

In the seventh century the Bedouins reached much further afield than usual. This was because they were inspired by the religious teachings of a new prophet, who urged them to fight a 'holy war' (*jihad*) to spread the new faith amongst 'unbelievers'. His name was Mohammed, and he was born about 570 in the dusty trading town of Mecca. For many years he worked as a merchant, often travelling north to Syria. He probably gained some knowledge of writing and counting in the course of his work.

Mecca was busy with camel caravans. It was also the centre of Arab religion. In its cube-shaped place of worship, called the *Kaaba*, stood statues of several hundred gods – spirits of the stars, rocks, winds and oases. It was a place of pilgrimage where, each spring, pilgrims came from all corners of Arabia to worship in the *Kaaba* and kiss the black stone embedded in one of its walls. This stone, probably a meteorite, was believed to have come from heaven.

Mohammed was troubled by this worshipping of gods and idols. He began to retreat to a quiet mountain cave, to think, fast and pray for long periods. He said that it was there that the Angel Gabriel appeared to him in a vision and revealed that there was only one god, *Allah*, and Mohammed was to be His Prophet. *Allah* was the same God as the God of the Jews and the Christians. But Mohammed said that the Angel told him he was to be the last in a long line of prophets, including Abraham, Moses and Jesus Christ. These prophets, although bearing God's message, were not themselves divine.

Mohammed started preaching, but his attacks on the Arabs' false gods angered the rulers of Mecca who threatened to silence him. Fortunately the Prophet's fame had spread to Medina, 250 miles (400 km) away. There many Jews and Arabs were attracted by his teachings. So in 622 Mohammed and a few faithful followers moved to Medina. This event, known as the *Hegira* (breaking of old ties), proved such a turning point that it became Year 1 in the Muslim calendar – just as Christ's birth marks the start of the Christian calendar.

The Meccans attacked Medina several times, and fierce battles

A mosque, like this one at Isfahan, in Iran (Persia), is a place where Muslims gather to worship Allah, under the direction of a prayer leader (they do not have priests)

were fought, during which the Prophet showed himself to be an able military commander. When the Prophet finally captured Mecca in 630 he destroyed the idols in the *Kaaba*, but not the building itself. He pardoned many of his enemies and as a result many of them became followers of his faith. When Mohammed died, two years later, most Arabs had accepted the new religion of *Islam* – meaning 'obedience to the will of God'. Those who 'obey' are called Muslims.

The Koran

The revelations that came to Mohammed were memorised and written down by his followers. They were put in order under his instructions, and compiled in their final form – in a book called the *Koran* – less than ten years after the Prophet's death. The text of the *Koran* is the same now as it was then. Nothing has been changed.

The *Koran* is the Holy Book of Muslims. It contains instructions on how a true Muslim should live and worship God. There are five basic 'Pillars' (rules) of Islam, which Muslims still follow:

1. The confession of faith: 'There is no God but *Allah* and Mohammed is His Prophet.'
2. Prayer: five times a day Muslims pray, facing the *Kaaba* (House of God) in Mecca.
3. Fasting: as an act of self-discipline all believers fast from dawn to sunset during *Ramadan*, the ninth month of the Muslim year.
4. Charity (*Zakah*): a certain part of a Muslim's income is given to the poor and homeless, and other Islamic causes.
5. Pilgrimage (*Hajj*): if possible, all Muslims must make a pilgrimage to Mecca once during their lifetime.

The *Koran* also urges believers to struggle for the spread of the true faith (*jihad*), if necessary by fighting. This 'holy war' was really aimed at heathens. Islam recognises the faith of the Jewish and Christian religions and gives them freedom to follow their own practices.

The *Koran* gave guidance to Muslims in their everyday lives. For instance, pork was declared unclean and forbidden; gambling and strong drinks were also forbidden, and the use of faulty weights and measures in trading was condemned. Instructions were given for the treatment of slaves and the care of wives. The *Koran* said a man may have up to four wives at any one time, provided he looked after them all in the same way. This custom arose in the days when there were more women than men, and many of them were left without a protector.

Mohammed promised to the faithful a Paradise where they might expect to dwell at ease in a 'cool garden of spreading shade, and water gushing, and fruit in plenty'. On the other hand, the 'evil and unbelieving' would go to hell, a place of 'scorching wind and scalding water and shadow of black smoke'.

The spread of Islam

United by faith as never before, the Arabs swept northwards conquering the lands of the Byzantine Empire, spreading Islam as they went. Mohammed had promised rewards in paradise for those who showed faith and courage:

> The sword is the key of heaven and hell; all who draw it in the cause of the faith will be rewarded . . . . If they fall in battle . . . they will be transported to paradise, there to revel in eternal pleasure.

Only six years after Mohammed's death (638) the Arabs had conquered Syria and thousands were making new homes there. Then, turning east, the swift Arab horsemen overran the Persian Empire with astonishing ease (637–44). Before long Muslims were crossing the frontiers of India and China.

Meanwhile, Egypt was conquered (642) and the Arabs began moving westwards along the North African coast. By 711 Muslim forces were crossing the Straits of Gibraltar into Spain. These were mostly Berbers (or Moors) from the Sahara desert, who had fought hard before accepting the faith of Islam. Now they quickly became masters of Spain.

Not until 717 were the armies of Islam seriously checked. Advancing through Asia Minor (now Turkey) they attacked Constantinople by land and sea. But after a bitter struggle the Byzantines forced them back and recovered most of Asia Minor. Soon afterwards the Moors in the West were also checked. They invaded France but in 732 they were beaten by the Franks, under their leader Charles Martel. The Franks drove the Moors back into Spain, where they remained for a further 700 years.

The power of the conquering armies of Islam had passed its

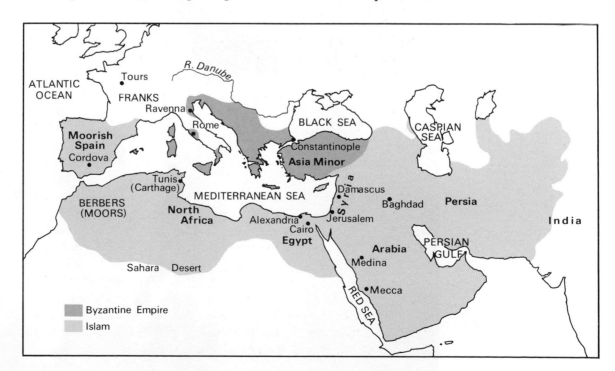

The world of Islam, about 732 – a century after the death of Mohammed

peak. But Islamic influence over the lands stretching from the Atlantic to the Himalayas remained. The Jewish and Christian populations had to pay taxes, although they were free to practise their religions. Most of the conquered peoples, however, became Muslims. Apart from Spain, these lands are still largely Muslim today.

After Mohammed's death the Islamic state was ruled by a *caliph* (deputy or successor). From about 750 onwards caliphs had their capital at Baghdad, a great city rivalling Constantinople in its

Part of the interior of the beautiful Selimyie Mosque in Nicosia, Cyprus

Part of Baghdad today

splendour. The caliph Al-Mansur planned the new city of Baghdad as the centre of the still expanding Muslim empire. One hundred thousand men built the so-called 'City of Peace' in only four years. The caliphs of Baghdad, however, soon found it impossible to rule the whole of the Islamic world. Distant provinces such as Moorish Spain therefore became self-governing.

Merchants and scholars

By breaking down frontiers, Muslims encouraged trade across three continents. In the crowded *bazaars* (markets) of cities such as Baghdad the rich could buy all kinds of luxury goods. There were jewels, silks, perfumes and spices from China and the Far East; decorated leather and glassware from North Africa and Egypt; furs from central Asia, and magnificent Persian carpets, tapestries and brocades. Arab traders even brought gold, ivory and ostrich feathers from tropical Africa, making the first real contacts between Negro peoples and the rest of the world.

Helped by the common language of Arabic, ideas travelled as easily as goods throughout Islam. The Arabs were quick to learn from the peoples they had conquered. Great writings from far and wide, especially those of ancient Greece, were translated and stored in vast libraries. Through trading with the Far East, Arabs learned about paper-making, the windmill, spinning wheel and magnetic compass.

These inventions later reached Europe, through Spain and Sicily. So did the nine 'Arabic' numerals that we still use today (they originally came from India). The zero, which allows numerals to be arranged in columns representing tens, hundreds and so on, possibly came first from the Chinese. However it was a ninth century Muslim, Al-Khawarizmi, who first described it in a book that has come down to us. He was also one of the inventors of algebra (*al-jabr* in Arabic).

Not only in mathematics but also in medical science Muslim scholars were far in advance of Europeans in the Middle Ages. They made important discoveries in the treatment of eye disorders, so common in the East. Al-Razi from Baghdad (865–925) wrote about 140 books on medicine, including the first scientific account of smallpox. Avicenna, who lived a century later, wrote a medical encyclopaedia which was the most complete collection of medical knowledge made anywhere in the Middle Ages.

Caliphs themselves often encouraged the work of scholars, poets, artists and musicians. Harun Al-Rashid (caliph 786–809) once gave 5,000 gold pieces, a horse and ten slave girls to a poet who wrote a sonnet in his honour. Harun is the hero in many tales of the *Arabian Nights*, a collection of about 200 stories of fantasy and adventure.

Page from a British edition of the Arabian Nights *printed in the early nineteenth century*

Sources and questions

1. Look at the picture on page 41.
   (a) Can you point out at least *three* ways by which we are able to identify the Emperor? What do you think he is holding?
   (b) What do the three men on the right of the picture have in common? Describe what each is holding. One has a special kind of haircut – what is it called?
   (c) What do the figures on the left of the picture tell us about Justinian's rule?
   (d) Ravenna is in northern Italy, a long way from Byzantium. Why would Justinian have been treated with such respect in a foreign land? (The map on page 42 may help you.)

2. One of the early Islamic conquests was the great Syrian city of Damascus, which surrendered in September 635 after six months' siege. The Arab general, Khālid ibn-al-Walid, offered the following terms:

   > In the name of Allah, the sympathetic, the merciful. This is what Khālid ibn-al-Walid would grant to the inhabitants of Damascus if he enters therein: he promises to give them security for their lives, property and churches. Their city wall shall not be demolished, neither shall any Muslim be quartered in their houses. So long as they pay the poll tax, nothing but good shall befall them.

   Adapted from P. K. Hitti, History of the Arabs, *Macmillan, 2nd Edition, 1940, page 156*

(a) A poll tax has to be paid equally by everyone. In this case it consisted of some money and a measure of wheat per head. Why do you think the victors chose this form of taxation?

(b) Why might the people of Damascus have feared that their city wall would be demolished?

(c) What was the point of offering such generous terms to the defeated?

(d) Why do you think the Arabs found this method of conquest successful?

3. In the year 640, the Arabs, outnumbered roughly two to one, overran an Egyptian army near Cairo in Egypt. After the battle, a spokesman for one of the Egyptian commanders, Cyrus, described the victorious Arabs as follows.

> We have witnessed a people to each and every one of whom death is preferable to life, . . . and to none of whom this world has the least attraction. They sit not except on the ground, and eat naught but on their knees. Their leader is like unto one of them: the low cannot be distinguished from the high, nor the master from the slave. And when the time of prayer comes none of them absents himself, all wash their extremities and humbly observe their prayer.

Adapted from P. K. Hitti, History of the Arabs, *Macmillan, 2nd Edition, 1940, page 163*

(a) Can you find anything in the teachings of Mohammed which would have made the Arab warriors unafraid of death?

(b) Why do you think the speaker mentions each of the following?
    i) The Arabs' ways of sitting and eating.
    ii) The difficulty of distinguishing the 'low' from the 'high'.
    iii) The Arabs' strict observance of prayers.

(c) Why do you think the defeated Egyptians made this statement?

(d) Does this document help you to understand more clearly the Arabs' military successes? Give reasons for your answer.

4. What do you think were the main differences between Christ and Mohammed as men? In what ways were they similar?

THE EMPEROR CHARLEMAGNE

It was the Franks who finally halted the advance of Islam in the West. At the battle of Tours (732) Charles Martel's cavalry crushed the Muslim invaders. But away from the battlefield the Franks (who gave their name to France) had much to learn from their opponents.

For centuries to come the Christian peoples of the West remained backward in comparison with their Muslim rivals. While the subjects of Islam grew rich through trade, constructed fine buildings and brought together knowledge from many lands, the Franks and their neighbours were mostly ignorant farming folk. They lived simple lives in small, isolated villages, knowing nothing of prosperous cities such as Baghdad, Damascus and Cordova.

With the exception of a few monks and priests, knowledge of reading and writing had almost died out among the Franks. In the sixth century, Bishop Gregory of Tours admitted he could not write Latin properly. Yet he took on the task of writing an early *History of the Franks* because he knew of no scholar 'sufficiently skilled in the art of writing' who could do it better. Improvement was slow in the next 200 years. Royal documents from this period, written in an ugly scrawl, show that even the king's clerks did not know basic rules of grammar.

The palace school at Aachen

The powerful Frankish kingdom was still very backward when Charles Martel's grandson became king in 768. He was also called Charles, but his achievements soon earned him the name *Charlemagne* (Charles the Great). The new king was strong and athletic. He loved riding, hunting and swimming, and, above all, he was a brave and skilful warrior. However, there was another, unusual, side to Charlemagne. He greatly enjoyed study and the company of scholars. Even at his dining table he listened thoughtfully to musicians, poets, or servants reading stories from history.

It shocked the King to find that many priests were so ignorant of Latin that they could neither write properly nor understand the Bible. He was not a scholar himself, but he believed it was a

Bronze statuette of Charlemagne cast in the ninth century

Picture of St Mark from a Gospel Book which was in use in the palace school, Aachen, at about the time of Charlemagne's death

Christian ruler's duty to educate his subjects. To set an example he started a school at his favourite palace at Aachen.

As teachers in the school Charlemagne wanted the best educated men of his day. This meant getting them from other countries – from Italy, Spain and, of course, England, where the scholars of Northumbria had earned a fine reputation. To the King's great delight, he was able to persuade Alcuin, master of York cathedral school, to come to his court and organise the teaching there.

Most pupils at the palace school were young men preparing to be priests. Their main studies were the Scriptures and the works of early Christian leaders. But first they were given a grounding in Latin. For this Alcuin and his companions had to write their own textbooks. At that time there were no books in the Frankish language, and most writings of the ancient Greeks were unknown in the West. So studies in language and literature were narrowed down to Latin.

againi...

Saxon resistance.

peaceful methods among ...

defeated them in 791 and advanced the

Na...
king...

'...
...

C...
...

Manuscript illustration
showing Alcuin

At a moment when Charlemagne's army was stretched out in a long column . . . these Basques, who had set their ambush on the very top of one of the mountains, came rushing down on the last part of the baggage train and on the troops who were marching in support of the rearguard and thus were protecting the army which had gone on ahead. The Basques forced them down into the valley beneath, joined battle with them and killed them to the last man. They then snatched up the baggage, and . . . scattered in all directions without losing a moment. In this feat the Basques were helped by the lightness of their arms and by the nature of the ground on which the battle was fought. On the other hand, the heavy nature of their own equipment and the unevenness of the ground completely hampered the Franks in their resistance.

Adapted from H. R. Loyn and J. Percival, Documents of Medieval History: The Reign of Charlemagne, *Edward Arnold, 1975, pages 13–14*

Oliver's climbed a hill above the plain,
Whence he can look on all the land of Spain,
And see how vast the Saracen array;
All those bright helms with gold and jewels gay,
And all those shields, those coats of burnished mail;
And all those lances from which the pennons wave;
Even their squadrons defy all estimate,
He cannot count them, their numbers are so great;
Stout as he is, he's mightily dismayed.
He hastens down as swiftly as he may,
Comes to the French and tells them all his tale.

'Quoth Oliver: "Huge are the Paynim hordes,
And of our French the numbers seem but small.
Companion Roland, I pray you sound your horn,
That Charles may hear and fetch back all his force."
Roland replies: "Madman were I and more,
And in fair France my fame would suffer scorn.
I'll smite great strokes with Durendal my sword,
I'll dye it red high as the hilt with gore.
This pass the Paynims reached on a luckless morn;
I swear to you death is their doom therefor.'

From The Song of Roland, *Penguin Classics, 1957 (translated by Dorothy L. Sayers), pages 91–2*

Questions

1. What do you think was the Basques' motive for the attack?
2. How does Einhard try to make excuses for the Frankish defeat?
3. Can you think of any similarities between *The Song of Roland* and the tales that have come down to us about the exploits of King Arthur in Britain?
4. How do the two sources differ concerning (**a**) the landscape, and (**b**) the army opposing the Franks?
5. In the poem, what does Roland say he would be a 'madman' to do? Does this fit in with Einhard's account?

Frankish knights ready for battle. Einhard thought their equipment 'heavy' in comparison with that of the Basques. Which items would he have had in mind?

Document 4

Einhard describes Charlemagne's determined attempts to improve his education.

> He was not content with his own mother tongue, but took the trouble to learn foreign languages. He learnt Latin so well that he spoke it as fluently as his own tongue; but he understood Greek better than he could speak it. . . .
>
> He paid the greatest attention to the creative arts, and he had great respect for men who taught them, bestowing high honours upon them. . . . He applied himself to mathematics and traced the course of the stars with great attention and care. He also tried to learn to write. With this object in view he used to keep writing-tablets and notebooks under the pillows on his bed, so that he could try his hand at forming letters during his leisure moments; but, although he tried very hard, he had begun too late in life and he made little progress.

Adapted from H. R. Loyn and J. Percival, Documents of Medieval History: The Reign of Charlemagne, *Edward Arnold, 1975, page 18*

Questions

1. Why was knowledge of Latin and Greek considered so important in Charlemagne's day?
2. The ability to trace the course of the stars was often put to practical use at this time. Can you explain how?
3. Is there any reason to believe that Charlemagne was embarrassed by his backwardness at writing?
4. What does this extract tell you about Einhard's attitude towards Charlemagne?
5. In Document 1 we see Charlemagne as a warrior. What different side to his character emerges from Document 4?

An example of minuscule writing. Why did Alcuin encourage its use?

An Anglo-Saxon king with his Witan, *or assembly of thanes. It seems that a wrongdoer has been condemned to death; we can see him being hanged on the right of the picture*

of the *kindred* (relatives). Nowadays we try to keep law and order by having police, prisons and so on. But in those days it was fear of the kindred that helped to prevent crime. If a man was killed, injured or wronged in any way, his kindred would either take revenge on the person responsible or claim compensation based on the wergeld.

Kings and church leaders encouraged the peaceful method of settlement, in money or goods. But if the wrongdoer would not, or could not, pay compensation, vengeance ('the blood feud') was the only alternative. Some crimes, such as betrayal of one's lord, were so serious that compensation was not enough. The penalty was death, usually by hanging. Other kinds of punishment, such as imprisonment, were rarely mentioned in the laws. However, if an accused man failed to appear and answer a charge against him he was declared an *outlaw* and could be killed by anyone.

The people held regular open-air meetings, or *folk-moots*, to deal with law-breakers, among other things. In law courts today both sides try to produce evidence about the facts of the case. But Anglo-Saxon customs were different. The *defendant* (the person accused) was usually asked to swear a solemn oath of innocence and then bring forward 'oath-helpers' to swear that the oath was true.

The value of oath-helpers depended on their rank. The word of a thane or bishop was worth much more than that of a churl. If enough of the right sort of oath-helpers were produced the case was over. Sometimes the right to swear an oath belonged to the other side – the *plaintiff*. This happened when the defendant was caught in the act or was a suspicious character who had been accused before.

If not enough oath-helpers could be found, the judgment usually depended upon *trial by ordeal*. A priest took charge and asked the defendant to choose either iron or water. In the ordeal of cold water the defendant was thrown into a pond or river. It was believed that the water would cast out the guilty, who floated, yet 'receive' the innocent, who sank!

The ordeal by iron was a 'burn test'. The defendant carried a red hot iron bar a short distance. The hand was then bandaged, and if the wound healed in three days without festering the defendant was declared innocent. Sometimes a burn test was done with boiling water. The defendant plunged a hand into it to take out a stone. The idea behind all these 'ordeals' was that God would give a judgment by helping only the innocent.

Farming and trading

Much of the countryside in this period was uninhabited. There were great stretches of moor, marshland and dense forest where wolves, wild boar and herds of deer roamed. Many of the English settlers took over lands cleared by the Britons. But in some places they began to tame the wilderness and establish new village communities. They made forest clearings, used the timber for building and for fuel, and divided up the land for farming.

The chief crops were cereals – barley, rye and wheat – which were made into bread. Barley was also used in brewing beer. Peas, beans and flax were often grown, and bees were kept. Honey was important because in those days people had no sugar, so it was the only kind of sweetening. On the wasteland bordering the village families kept a few cattle, sheep or pigs.

Most villages had a 'lord' – one of the king's thanes – whom the people looked to for protection. The lord had a good share of the land and the villagers farmed it for him. Besides giving this free labour they paid regular 'food rent', in wheat, pigs, eggs and so on, which they carried up to the lord's hall.

Not all villagers farmed the land. Some carried on the necessary trades. Smiths made tools and other implements, including ploughs, shovels, pots and pans; and there were also carpenters,

Anglo-Saxon farming implements (a scythe blade and a small pickaxe head) and early pottery, dating from around the sixth century

Artist's impression of an English soldier at the time of Alfred

the 'joys of the hall'. But when he was nearly forty years old he began to learn reading and writing, with the help of Bishop Asser. The King must have studied hard because after about five years he could write fairly good English and Latin.

Up to Alfred's time *Englisc*, as he called it, was mainly a spoken language. Songs, stories and poems were learned and recited, but few seem to have been written down. The laws of kings had to be written in English, because they were for all the people, not just the educated. But books were in Latin – the language of scholars and churchmen. Now Alfred decided it was time for a change. He wanted to translate important books into English. Then the sons of his thanes, who one day would help to govern the kingdom, could be taught to read in 'the language we can all understand'.

Among the books translated by the King and his scholars were Gregory the Great's *Pastoral Rule*, Bede's *History of the English Church and People*, and *Universal History*, written by a Roman called Orosius in the fifth century. Alfred played a large part in this work. In the front of the *Pastoral Rule* it says: 'King Alfred translated every word of me into English.'

History was one of Alfred's special interests. He got scholars to find out all they could about the history of the English since the earliest settlements. Monastery records were collected, and also songs and stories that had been passed from one generation to the next. Then the *Anglo-Saxon Chronicle* was written – a kind of diary, but in years rather than days. For the earlier centuries it is little more than a register of kings and battles. But when it gets to Alfred's time the Chronicle is often very detailed.

Copies of the *Anglo-Saxon Chronicle* were sent to a number of monasteries, where they were kept up to date. Seven different versions have been discovered, one of them continuing up to 1154. They all tell much the same story, although occasionally they contradict each other. From Alfred's reign onwards the Chronicles are very accurate because events were recorded at the time they were happening.

In 899 the chroniclers had sad news to report: 'In this year Alfred son of Ethelwulf died, six days before All Saints' Day'. The Chronicle itself and Alfred's own writings were his greatest memorial to future ages. He left many fine buildings as well – royal halls, new churches and monasteries. We also remember Alfred through his Code of Laws. In this he tried to give protection to his poorer and weaker subjects, who were often harshly treated by powerful landowners. No one summed up Alfred's life better than the King himself, when he wrote: 'I desired to live worthily . . . and to leave after my life . . . my memory in good works'.

Re-conquest of the Danelaw

Alfred's kingdom passed to his son, Edward 'the Elder'. He was an experienced soldier and he set out to increase the power of Wessex. His main aim was to conquer the Danelaw – the lands where the Danes had settled in eastern England. The Mercians,

Tenth century artist's impression of King Athelstan presenting St Cuthbert with the Venerable Bede's book of the saint's life

who no longer had a king of their own, fought on Edward's side. They were led by his sister Ethelfleda, who was known as the 'First Lady of the Mercians'.

The English made a two-pronged advance into the Danelaw; Edward from the south and Ethelfleda from the west. Like mice nibbling at cheese they conquered the land in small stages. In each newly-won area a *burh* was constructed, just like those Alfred had built to protect Wessex.

The Danes offered little serious resistance. By this time many had settled down and were prepared to accept Edward as their king, provided they could go on farming in peace. This suited Edward. By 920 the conquest of the Danelaw was almost complete. The Danes were converted to Christianity, and churches and monasteries were built, often at places where earlier abbeys had been destroyed by the Great Army.

At the end of Edward's reign (925) all the English in the South and Midlands looked to him as their king. Edward's son Athelstan carried on where his father had left off. He took firm control of northern England, and even invaded Scotland. In 937 Athelstan was attacked by a large force of Scots, Britons and Norse settlers. But he crushed them in a great battle at Brunanburh, somewhere in Northumbria. According to the *Anglo-Saxon Chronicle*, 'Never before in this island . . . was an army put to greater slaughter by the sword since the Angles and Saxons came here.'

Athelstan now called himself *Rex Totius Britannae* (King of all

An extract from the Anglo-Saxon Chronicle, which is preserved in the British Museum, London. Here some of the Danish invasions are described – in English very different from that we speak today!

Britain) on his coins. His fame as a warrior had already spread far beyond the British Isles. Kings and dukes on the Continent sent him messages of friendship and beautiful gifts of gold and silver ornaments, weapons and decorated books. Athelstan gave richly in return.

The kingdom of England, therefore, grew out of the kingdom of Wessex. The Danes had helped to make this possible, although they did not realise it at the time. They destroyed the other kingdoms and so cleared the way for the union of all the English under a single king. Several centuries passed before the northern border with Scotland was fixed. But a start was made by King Edgar (959–75). He gave all the lands north of the River Tweed to Kenneth, king of the Scots. The Tweed still forms part of the Border today.

Shires, hundreds and towns

Once the Danelaw had been conquered it was divided into *shires*, many of them centred round towns, such as Derby, Nottingham or Leicester. Shires had already been formed in most other parts of England. Some of the southern ones, including Kent and Sussex, began as separate kingdoms. Nowadays we call these local divisions counties. Some of them still have the boundaries that were fixed in Anglo-Saxon times.

Each shire had its law court or *shire moot*, which met twice a year to deal with serious crimes and disputes. It was attended by important landowners, and a royal official called an *ealdorman* was in charge. He was the king's representative in that area. Among his other duties he had to call up and lead the shire forces in wartime.

In return for their service to the king, ealdormen (later called eorls) were given money and large estates. Some became very powerful nobles, controlling several shires at once. Their ordinary duties in each shire were given over to a shire-reeve, or *sheriff*. By the eleventh century one or two eorls were strong enough to challenge the power of the Crown. One of them, Harold Godwin, actually became king for a time in 1066.

Ordinary villagers helped to run affairs in their own district. Shires were divided into smaller areas called hundreds, which probably at first contained 100 'hides' or households. In each there was a monthly meeting called the *hundred moot*, where criminals were brought to justice. Commands from the king were read out by the leader of the meeting, known as the 'hundred man'.

There were also *burh moots* in the towns. This reminds us that many English towns grew up at places where Alfred, Edward the Elder and Ethelfleda built burhs for defence against the Danes. The protection given by these walled strongholds attracted merchants and craftsmen. They wanted market places where they could store and sell their goods in safety.

Other towns grew up at harbours, crossroads, or beside cathedrals such as Canterbury and York. London had long been the

Artist's impression of an ealdorman from the late Anglo-Saxon period

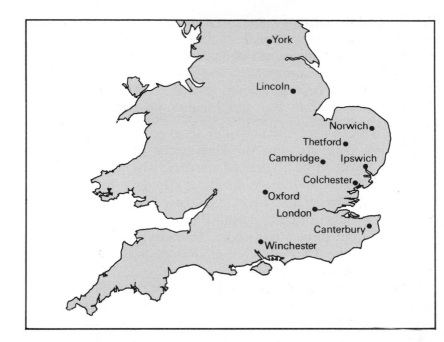

The main towns in England a thousand years ago. Notice that most grew up in the areas of Danish settlement. The Danes preferred to live in larger communities than the English. Apart from London, none of these towns is among the largest thirty in England today

main centre of shipping and overseas trade. It received cargoes of wine, fish, timber and pepper, and exported wool, cheese and iron goods. Even in the eighth century Bede had described London as '. . . the market of many nations, coming to it by sea and land'.

These places were very different from modern towns. They looked more like overgrown villages, bordered by farmland where corn grew and cattle grazed. Some town dwellers earned their living from the land. But most were merchants, clerks or craftsmen. One thing that would strike us about Anglo-Saxon towns would be the large number of churches. By the eleventh century there were about twenty in Norwich – roughly one for every 300 people. Churches were built of stone. So were the halls belonging to great nobles. But the houses of ordinary citizens were made of wood and thatch.

Experts can only give a rough estimate of the size of these towns. London, the biggest, probably had a population of more than 10,000 by the eleventh century. York and Winchester probably come next, each with over 8,000 citizens. Winchester had long been the chief city of Wessex. The king's main treasure was kept there. But it would be wrong to think of Winchester, or London, as the 'capital' of England. The king and his court still travelled around the country, and the Witan could meet on any of the royal estates.

The return of the Vikings

After the English had enjoyed a century of peace under strong kings, the dreaded dragon-heads of Viking ships were again seen along the coasts. This is how the *Anglo-Saxon Chronicle* described the early raids:

980 . . . Southampton was ransacked by a naval force, and

Coin depicting Cnut

Coin from the reign of Ethelred. Thousands of these were used to pay Danegeld

most of the citizens killed or taken captive; and in that same year Thanet was ravaged.

981 . . . great damage was done everywhere by the coast both in Devon and Cornwall.

982 . . . three ships of Vikings arrived in Dorset and ravaged in Portland. That same year London was burnt down.

These attacks were made by quite small groups of adventurers. But before long Scandinavian kings came in person, leading powerful armies of highly-trained warriors. The English were no match for them, and brave stands at Maldon, in Essex, and London ended in defeat. Things might have been different if there had been another Alfred to defend England. The king, Ethelred, was not cut out to be a war-leader. Nowadays he is remembered as Ethelred 'the Unready', but in fact he was known as the *Unraed*, which meant 'without good advice'.

Instead of fighting, Ethelred collected extra taxes and bribed the invaders to go away with large sums of money called *Danegeld* (Dane-payment). The Viking leaders rewarded their warriors and sailed away. But they were soon back for more. Still Ethelred preferred to pay rather than fight. According to the *Anglo-Saxon Chronicle*,

When the enemy were in the east, the English army was kept in the west, and when they were in the south, our army was in the north . . . Finally there was no leader willing to collect an army, but each fled as best as he could.

Year after year the Vikings seemed content to come just for *Danegeld*. But finally Swein 'Forkbeard', King of Denmark, decided to conquer England. In 1013 he landed in the North with a large army. Ethelred escaped across the Channel and Swein took the crown. But he was only king for a few weeks. He collapsed and fell dead off his horse in February 1014.

Ethelred came back, but he soon faced an army led by Swein's son Cnut (sometimes spelt Canute). By the end of 1016 Ethelred was dead, and so was his son Edmund 'Ironside', who had fought bravely against the invaders. Tired of the struggle, the English accepted Cnut as their king. He was only twenty years old.

King Cnut

Cnut was a strong and courageous young man. He could also be cruel. He had grown up in a hard world, surrounded by violence and bloodshed. So he did not hesitate to order the deaths of leading Englishmen he could not trust. Cnut's subjects feared him, but in time they also learned to respect him as a king who ruled firmly and justly.

To give himself a link with the English royal family, Cnut married Emma, Ethelred's widow. Then he set out to restore peace. He sent most of his fleet back to Denmark, after paying them off with the largest *Danegeld* ever collected in England –

This illustration from an eleventh century manuscript shows King Cnut and Queen Emma presenting a gift to the new cathedral at Winchester

82,500 pounds of silver. Cnut kept forty ships, and also a few of his best soldiers who became the King's *housecarls* (bodyguards).

Once his position was secure, Cnut called together a great assembly of nobles and Church leaders. He promised to rule fairly and to keep the laws of Edgar (who reigned before Ethelred). Although he gave lands to some of his Danish followers, many English nobles were allowed to keep their estates and positions of power. Cnut also promised to help the Christian faith. True to his word he built fine stone churches and even went on a pilgrimage to Rome in 1027.

For most of his nineteen-year reign Cnut was King of Denmark as well as England. And for a short time he ruled Norway and part of Sweden too. At least the English were safe from Viking attacks while Cnut reigned! When he died, in 1035, he left two sons – Harold and Harthacnut. It seemed his family was well established on the English throne. Yet only seven years later both sons were dead and Cnut's great North Sea empire had broken up.

The English crown went to Edward, son of Ethelred and a descendant of the kings of Wessex. He had grown up in Normandy, where he was taken for safety during Ethelred's reign. Edward knew less about England than the Danish kings he followed. But he was the great, great, great grandson of Alfred. That was enough to win him the support of the people.

*Coins depicting Cnut's sons:
(top) Harold 'Harefoot'
(below) Harthacnut*

Timeline

AD

899	Death of Alfred the Great
900–920	Re-conquest of the Danelaw (Edward 'the Elder')
937	Athelstan wins battle of Brunanburh
980	Viking invasions resumed
1013	Swein 'Forkbeard' conquers England
1016–35	Reign of King Cnut

Sources and questions

1. After he had translated Gregory the Great's *Pastoral Rule* from Latin into English, King Alfred sent a copy to each of his bishops. It contained an introduction, written by the King, from which the following extract is taken.

    Before everything was ransacked and burned, the churches throughout England stood filled with treasures and books. Similarly, there was a great multitude of those serving God. And they gained very little benefit from those books, because they could understand nothing of them, since they were not written in their own language . . . Therefore it seems better to me – if it seems so to you – that we should turn into the language that we can all understand certain books which are the most necessary for all men to know, . . . so that all the free-born young men now in England who have the means to apply themselves to it, may be set to learning (as long as they are not useful for some other employment) until the time that they can read English writings properly. Thereafter one may instruct in Latin those whom one wishes to teach further and wishes to advance to holy orders.

Adapted from S. Keynes and P. Lapidge, Alfred the Great – Contemporary Sources, *Penguin, 1983, pages 125–6*

(a) What do you think was Alfred's purpose in writing in this way to his bishops?
(b) Do you think the King exaggerates to suit his argument?
(c) What 'other employment' might Alfred have considered more important for young men even than learning to read? Do you agree with the King?
(d) Why would churchmen and scholars still need to understand Latin?

2. What were the similarities and differences between Alfred the Great and Charles the Great (Charlemagne)?

3. Here is part of the *Anglo-Saxon Chronicle's* entry for 1006.

1006 . . . Then after midsummer the Danish fleet came to Sandwich, and did just as they were accustomed: they ravaged, burned and killed as they went. Then the King ordered the whole of the people of Wessex and Mercia to be called out, and they were on military service against the Danish army all autumn, but with no more success than very often in the past; for, in spite of it all, the Danish army went about as it pleased, and the English fighting men caused the people of the country every sort of harm, so that they profited neither from the home army nor from the foreign invaders.

Adapted from Everyman Classics, 2nd Edition, 1972 (translated by G.N. Garmonsway), page 136

(a) What is the writer's attitude to these events?
(b) Why does the *Chronicle* describe the English army as being 'called out'? In what sense would the army have been 'the whole of the people'?
(c) How might the English army have caused harm to its own people?
(d) The King [Ethelred] is generally blamed for the failure to expel the Danes in this period. Does this account suggest any other possible reasons for the Danish supremacy?

4. Imagine you were living during Ethelred's reign in a part of England that was raided by the Danes. In the style of a modern newspaper report, write an 'eyewitness account' of the attack in about 200–300 words.

THE NORMAN CONQUEST

In the French town of Bayeux there is an exhibition gallery not far from the cathedral. Preserved in a glass frame around its walls is the world's most famous piece of needlework. It is a long strip of tapestry, made over 900 years ago. In a series of seventy-two pictures it shows how Duke William of Normandy conquered England in 1066. We see men feasting, hunting, fighting and dying, castles and ships being built, and action-packed battle scenes.

The pictures have Latin sub-titles. So the Bayeux tapestry is a kind of strip-cartoon and chronicle combined. It was probably made by English women, soon after 1066, at the orders of William's half-brother, Bishop Odo of Bayeux. The pictures were embroidered in eight colours of wool thread on pieces of linen. Then they were sewn together in a strip 70 metres long and 50 centimetres wide. A few pictures at the end have been lost. But it is still remarkable that a delicate tapestry should have survived while many stone buildings from this period have long since fallen into ruins.

The hero of the story, William 'the Conqueror', was descended from Rollo the Viking, who became the first duke of Normandy in 911 (see Chapter 7). Like his forefathers, William was tough, courageous and had a spirit of adventure. His army was the very last to invade and conquer England. That is why 1066 is a date the English remember.

Rivals for the crown

As the year 1065 drew to a close, King Edward of England lay dying in his London palace. His reign of more than twenty-three years had not been a happy one. Edward was a shy, peace-loving man. He sometimes lacked the necessary firmness to keep control of his powerful nobles. As a young man he gave most of his time to hunting and other pleasures. In the later years of his reign he became more religious, spending many hours praying and confessing his sins. To his subjects, Edward, who later became known as 'the Confessor', may have seemed more like a monk than a king.

The nobles and bishops of the King's Council (or Witan) gathered in London for the Christmas court of 1065. But the festivities

King Edward 'the Confessor', as shown in the Bayeux tapestry

Norman cavalry charging some of Harold's housecarls, who put up a shield wall. Both sides are throwing spears

to turn away, as though in retreat. Each time some Englishmen were drawn forward only to be surrounded and massacred.

Gaps now appeared in the wall of English shields. Late in the day the Normans finally broke through and Harold himself was killed. Looking at the Bayeux tapestry, it might seem that an arrow pierced his eye. But some historians argue that the man tugging at the arrow is one of the King's housecarls and that Harold is next to him, being hacked down by a Norman knight.

King Harold's reign of forty weeks was over, and so was one of the most important battles in the history of Europe. As darkness fell, the remains of the English army fled. They had fought with great courage, but in the end the better equipped and more disciplined side had won.

The death of King Harold. Historians still argue about whether he is the man with the arrow in his eye or the one being struck down by a Norman knight. Above, we see the Latin words Harold Rex Interfectus Est *(King Harold is killed)*

From Duke to King

The throne was vacant and within William's reach. But the Duke was not yet master of England. The powerful northern earls, Edwin and Morcar, had not fought in the great battle. William did not know whether they would try to stop him from being king. And he was not sure whether the people of London would resist him.

William did not march directly to London. He took a roundabout route, forcing the surrender of some important towns on the way (see map on page 98). At Canterbury the Duke fell ill, and his advance was halted for a month. The English might have taken this opportunity to raise a fresh army, but they seemed afraid of William and unable to agree on a new leader. The only serious resistance to the Conqueror came when he reached London Bridge. Rather than try to take the narrow wooden bridge by force, William decided to encircle London and approach it from the north.

The Normans crossed the Thames at Wallingford, where there was a shallow ford and bridge. By the time they reached Berkhamsted the Londoners had decided to surrender. A party of leading Englishmen, including Edwin, Morcar and the rulers of the Church, met William and agreed to accept him as King. To make sure no one changed their minds, he ordered his soldiers to burn and destroy the surrounding countryside along the way from Berkhamsted to London.

On Christmas Day 1066 the Duke was crowned King William I at Westminster Abbey. Like rulers before him, he swore to govern justly. Although he had gained the crown by force, he did not want his new subjects to think of him as a foreign conqueror. He claimed to be the rightful king – the first choice of Edward the Confessor. And he announced that Edward's laws must still be kept.

Artist's impression of a motte and bailey castle. Such wooden buildings perished long ago, but mounds and ditches of these castles can still be seen in many parts of England and France

attack. But if the ground was flat a great mound of earth called a *motte* was made, leaving a deep ditch all round. On top of the motte a stockade (wall of wooden stakes) was built and, inside this, a wooden tower or *keep*.

Beside the motte there was a kind of yard or enclosure called a *bailey*. This too was surrounded by a stockade, bank and ditch. Inside were living quarters, kitchens, storage huts, stables and workshops. (The keep was normally occupied only when the castle was under attack.) All the back-breaking work of digging, cutting timber and putting up the buildings was done by English peasants.

No baron could build a castle for himself without the King's permission. William wanted to be sure that all castles were in the hands of trusted men who would not rebel. Some of his most loyal supporters were given the task of building royal castles and guarding them for the King. Royal castles were built in all the main towns, to keep order and to provide safe bases for county sheriffs. If the best site for such a castle was already occupied by houses these were knocked down and families made homeless. In Lincoln, 166 houses were destroyed to make room for a royal castle.

Before long the Normans were busy strengthening their castles with stone walls round the motte and bailey. These were more difficult to break down than wooden stockades, and they could not be set on fire. The wooden keep on the motte usually remained. The result was a *shell-keep* – a wooden building inside protected by a hard outer ring or 'shell' of stone.

Despite this extra protection, attackers found ways of breaking into shell-keeps. If there was a *moat* (a water-filled ditch crossed only by a drawbridge) they built a crossing with stones, earth and wood. Then they brought up ladders and wooden *siege towers*,

which were tall enough for men on top to shoot arrows over the wall. Sometimes the attackers tried to make a hole in the wall. Huge boulders were fired from machines like catapults, and battering-rams were used. These were iron-tipped tree-trunks, which swung on chains between posts.

In defence, the castle guards fired showers of arrows, dropped stones and tried to set fire to ladders, siege towers and other equipment. If the attackers failed to break into the castle they might camp nearby and try to starve out the defenders by cutting off supplies from outside. This could take a long time, because a castle usually had its own well for water and ample storage space for food.

By far the strongest Norman castles were *stone keeps* or 'great towers', usually square in shape. One of the first of these was the White Tower, built by William in London to guard the approach to the city up the Thames. Other buildings have been added since the Conqueror's day, making up what we call the Tower of London. The massive Norman keep still stands in the centre, nearly 30 metres high with walls up to 5 metres thick.

William also had stone keeps at Exeter and Colchester. But most castles of this type were built in the next century. The Conqueror's youngest son, Henry I, built several – including the one pictured on page 109, at Rochester. On the ground floor of a stone keep food and weapons were stored and prisoners locked in dungeons. The main entrance was usually above, on the first floor, reached by an outside flight of steps. This led into a great hall, the main room of the castle. Meals were eaten in the hall, and at night the guards slept there.

Stone keeps were dark, draughty places to live in. But they were built for safety rather than comfort. The windows were narrow

The earthworks of a motte and bailey castle at Pleshey in Essex are still clearly visible in this photograph

The White Tower – the keep of the Tower of London. It was built by the Normans between 1078 and 1090, on the site of an earlier wooden castle put up as soon as William arrived in London

in front of his lord, a sword and spurs were fastened on and he swore to be loyal, brave and well-mannered.

How did the coming of the Normans affect ordinary peasants? After 1066 there were fewer *freeholders* – men who rented land without having to give services in return. But the lives of most country folk hardly changed. Instead of serving an English thane, peasants served a French-speaking lord of the manor (see Chapter 16). Not until the thirteenth and fourteenth centuries were peasants expected to do military service in any large numbers. By then there was a need for bigger armies, containing many footsoldiers.

Domesday Book

At Christmas 1085 William called his usual Great Council of barons and bishops. The *Anglo-Saxon Chronicle*, still kept going by the monks of Peterborough, tells us that

> the King had much thought and very deep speech with his Council about this land – how it was peopled and with what sort of men.

The stone keep built by Henry I at Rochester in Kent. Notice how it dominates the crossing of the river Medway. It is about 40 metres high and has four floors inside (one more than the White Tower in London)

In future, instead of guessing he wanted to know exactly how much land each tenant held and what taxes he could expect. He ordered that a detailed survey of England should be made without delay.

Royal officials were sent round the kingdom to find out about every village. They wanted to know who was the lord and who had owned the land before the Conquest, what the land was worth and how much of it was ploughland, meadow, pasture and woodland. They also wrote down the number of freeholders, *villeins* (ordinary peasants) and *bordars* (poorer peasants). Even watermills, fishponds and livestock were counted.

Here is part of the account of Birmingham, then a tiny village:

Richard holds Bermingeham of William (William FitzAnsculf, a tenant-in-chief) . . . There is land for 6 ploughs; there is one plough in the *demesne* (Richard's private land). There are 5 villeins and 4 bordars and 2 ploughs. There is a wood half a mile long and 4 furlongs broad. In the time of King Edward it was worth 20 shillings, and it is still worth the same.

The survey was finished before the end of 1086, and hundreds of parchment sheets were taken to the King. He did not study

The two large volumes which make up Domesday Book. They are kept in the Public Record Office, London. Thanks to this great survey we know more about England under the Normans than in any earlier period

them long as he was about to leave for Normandy. Royal clerks arranged the information under counties and finally made up two great volumes which came to be called *Domesday Book*. Domesday means the Day of Judgment. The book got this name because the facts in it could not be ignored or avoided by anyone, like the Judgment Day.

Accounts of a few towns, including London, have not been found. Nevertheless, for the first time we can work out England's total population fairly accurately. It was about $1\frac{1}{2}$ million in 1086 – roughly equal to the combined populations of Birmingham and Liverpool today. Domesday Book also shows the effects of the Norman Conquest. County by county, a new ruling class of foreigners had replaced the English thanes.

The Conqueror's sons

William never saw Domesday Book in its finished form. He met his death in the summer of 1087, while fighting the King of France. He was riding through the French town of Mantes, which his army had set on fire, when his horse trod on a smouldering piece of wood. It shied and threw the sixty-year old King heavily against the iron *pommel* (knob) on the front of his saddle. William was seriously injured and died a month later (9 September).

Extract from an illustrated manuscript, showing, on the left, King Henry I at sea

The Conqueror is remembered for his courage, determination and skill as a king. He was also hard and cruel. He humbled the English thanes, harried the North, demanded heavy taxes and made harsh forest laws to protect his animals from poachers. Any man who killed a deer had his eyes put out. Hunting was William's greatest joy, and he increased the size of the royal forests. In Hampshire, many villages were destroyed and families made homeless when a large area of woodland and rough pasture was taken over for the King's sport. Today it is still called the New Forest.

The Conqueror divided his lands and wealth between his three sons. Henry, the youngest, got £5,000 in silver. Robert, the eldest, became duke of Normandy. The English crown went to William, the second son and his father's favourite. William II was short, fat and red-faced, which explains his nickname 'Rufus' (Latin for red). When he got angry or excited he stuttered so badly that no one could understand him. Rufus was harsh and unpopular but a strong king. His subjects were afraid to disobey him.

In August 1100, Rufus was mysteriously killed by an arrow while hunting in the New Forest. His companions said it was an accident, but it might have been murder. William's brother Henry was quick to seize the royal treasure at Winchester and ride to London, where he was crowned only three days after Rufus's death. As a man, Henry I was cruel and greedy. But he was a firm and wise ruler. For thirty-five years he gave England order and justice.

In the powerful grip of the Conqueror and his sons England went through many changes. The close link with Normandy resulted in more trade and travel across the Channel. New ideas were introduced from Europe, including fighting on horseback. And a new language – Norman French – was brought to England by William and his followers. In time many French words crept into the English still spoken by ordinary peasants.

Under bishops and abbots from the Continent the English Church became stricter. Monks kept more closely to their vows, and priests were better educated. Within a century the Normans rebuilt many parish churches and most of the country's cathedrals and abbeys. Numerous old churches in England still have traces of Norman stone-work: rounded arches, thick walls and huge pillars. Such buildings were massive and very strong – like the Normans themselves.

Sources and questions

1. This writer of the *Anglo-Saxon Chronicle* who, we are told, lived for a time in William I's court, had this to say about the Conqueror in the year of his death.

   1087 . . . King William was . . . stronger than any king before. He was gentle to the good men who loved God, and stern beyond all measure to those who disobeyed him. . . . Amongst other things the good peace he made in this land is not to be forgotten – so that any honest man could travel over his kingdom unharmed with his pockets full of gold.
   . . . He caused castles to be built
     Which were a heavy burden to the poor.
     A hard man was the King
     And took from his subjects many marks (coins)
     In gold and many more hundreds of pounds in silver
   . . . Most unjustly and for little need . . . .
     The rich complained and the poor were full of
       sorrow,
     But he was too pitiless to care even though all might
       hate him.

   Adapted from Everyman Classics, 2nd Edition, 1972 (translated by G.N. Garmonsway), pages 219–21

   (a) Can you find any indications in this extract that the writer had once observed the King in his court?
   (b) Do you think it is fair to say that William was 'stern beyond all measure' to those who opposed him? Give reasons for your views.
   (c) How might the building of castles have been a 'burden to the poor'?
   (d) What is the chronicler's main criticism of William's rule? What do you think the King would have said in answer to this criticism – how would he have justified his actions?

Part of the interior of Gloucester Cathedral, showing rounded Norman arches and massive pillars

2. Imagine you are a baron who has decided to build a castle in your town or village. Suggest *three* suitable sites, and explain why you think each is a good defensive position.

3. Make a 'Glossary of Feudalism', including the meanings of such terms as tenant-in-chief, under-tenant, villein, homage, manor, page, squire and demesne.

4. In this scene from the early part of the Bayeux tapestry, we see a Norman attack on a motte and bailey castle at Dinan in France.

(a) Find the motte and describe what has been built on top of it.

(b) Using this picture and the one on page 104, can you work out how the attackers have got across the gap between the bailey and the motte?

(c) By what method are the attackers trying to destroy the castle? Why would it often have been effective in this period?

(d) Describe the weapons and armour of the soldiers on both sides.

HENRY II AND THOMAS BECKET

Coin showing King Stephen (1135–54). He was brave and honourable, but he failed to stop the lawlessness in his kingdom. A chronicler described his reign as 'nineteen long winters'

One moonlit night in 1120 a fine vessel called *The White Ship* was crossing the Channel from Normandy to England. On board was Prince William, son of Henry I, along with many barons and ladies of noble birth. The sea was calm and the passengers in good spirits. But suddenly there was a crashing and jolting. The ship had struck a rock and a gaping hole was torn in its wooden hull. Only one man, a servant, lived to tell the tale.

The loss of *The White Ship* had tragic results for England. It meant Henry I had no son to rule after him. Before his death, in 1135, he named his daughter Matilda as the heir to the throne. But the idea of a woman ruler was not popular, and Matilda was proud and domineering. A large group of barons gave their support to Henry's nephew, Count Stephen, who was crowned king.

Matilda stood up for her rights and gathered an army to fight Stephen. The outcome was civil war, with the powerful men in the kingdom taking sides. Some barons saw the chance to increase their wealth by robbery and murder. They built castles without the King's permission and rode about the countryside with their own private armies. Stephen was so busy fighting his enemies that the government of England was neglected. Men openly broke the laws and escaped punishment. The peace and order established by the Conqueror and his sons was shattered.

The first of the Plantagenets

After years of misery and bloodshed the two sides made a bargain. It was agreed that Stephen should reign as long as he lived, but Matilda's son, Henry, would be the next king. Within a year Stephen was dead. Henry sailed from France and was crowned at Westminster in December 1154. He was twenty-one years old; stocky, broad-shouldered and slightly bow-legged from much horse-riding. He had watchful grey eyes and dark red hair, closely cropped.

Henry II was the first of a long line of 'Plantagenet' kings, so called because the yellow broom flower (*planta genesta*) was the badge of his father, Geoffrey of Anjou. By the standards of the twelfth century Henry was well educated. He could read and

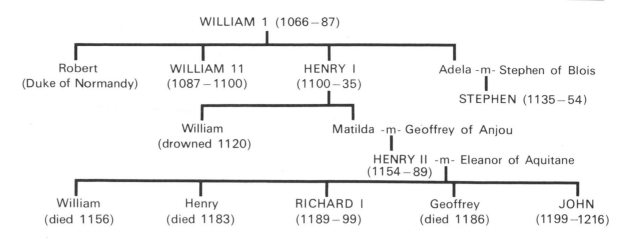

WILLIAM 1 (1066—87)

Robert
(Duke of Normandy)

WILLIAM 11
(1087—1100)

HENRY I
(1100—35)

Adela -m- Stephen of Blois

STEPHEN (1135—54)

William
(drowned 1120)

Matilda -m- Geoffrey of Anjou

HENRY II -m- Eleanor of Aquitane
(1154—89)

William
(died 1156)

Henry
(died 1183)

RICHARD I
(1189—99)

Geoffrey
(died 1186)

JOHN
(1199—1216)

Family tree of the Kings of England, 1066—1216

write, and it was said that he had some knowledge of every language spoken from France to Palestine. However, he only knew French and Latin well. Although he could read English he never learned to speak it properly.

Nothing seemed to tire Henry. He worked far into the night yet was often busy again soon after dawn. He loved hunting and would ride all day until he was sore and blistered from the saddle. Such great energy made him hard to live with. According to Walter Map, a member of Henry's household, the King was always moving from one palace or castle to the next:

> Tolerant of the discomforts of dust and mud . . . [Henry] was always on the move, travelling in unbearably long stages . . . and merciless beyond measure to the household that accompanied him.

Sometimes Henry gave his servants just a few hours to pack all the valuables, clothes, food, bedding, weapons and equipment of the entire court! Members of his household complained that he never sat down, except to eat. Even then he was busy reading a book, writing or discussing matters of government with his advisers.

Henry needed all his strength and energy, because he had vast possessions to govern. Besides England, he ruled more than half of France. The northern French lands were inherited from his father and mother, except for Brittany which he gained later. The lands in southern France, stretching down to the Spanish border, came to him as a result of his marriage, in 1152, to Eleanor, Countess of Aquitaine. Eleanor was more than ten years older than Henry. She was a lively, quick-witted woman, and must have greatly influenced the young King in the early part of his reign.

King Henry II's empire. Henry was supposed to hold all his French lands as a tenant-in-chief of the King of France. He did his rightful homage to King Louis VII, but, like the Norman kings before him, he was more powerful than his feudal overlord and never took orders from him

Henry restores order

England was again under a strong king, after nineteen years of lawlessness. Henry declared that every castle built in Stephen's reign must be destroyed. Within a year about 300 illegal castles were burned or pulled down. Meanwhile Henry sent home many foreign knights who had been hired by one side or the other during

Sixteenth century picture of pilgrims leaving the walled city of Canterbury

in the fourteenth century by the poet Geoffrey Chaucer. English was then beginning to replace Latin in the writing of stories and poems, although the language Chaucer used was different from our English today.

The poet tells how a party of thirty pilgrims set out from London to visit Becket's shrine. To pass the time, they tell each other stories as they ride along. These make up the bulk of Chaucer's poem, but he also describes each of the pilgrims. He must have been on a journey of this kind himself and drawn his characters from real life. Among them are people of many different occupations – a much-travelled knight and his squire, a merchant, a friar, an Oxford scholar, a miller, priest, cook, doctor, monk and many more.

Chaucer's opinion of his religious characters is very interesting. He admired the priest because he practised what he preached. He had few possessions, 'But riche he was of hooly thoght and werk'. However, Chaucer poked fun at the other churchmen because they did not live as strictly as they should. The fat monk was fonder of the hunting field than of the cloister:

Chaucer on his horse – from an illustrated manuscript of The Canterbury Tales. Geoffrey Chaucer (1340–1400) was the son of a London merchant. For a time he worked in the service of King Edward III. He travelled abroad, and was once a Member of Parliament for the county of Kent. His wide experience helped him to become one of England's greatest poets

Popular places of pilgrimage in England

a **Westminster Abbey**
Shrine of King Edward the Confessor – made a saint in the twelfth century.

b **Canterbury Cathedral**
Shrine of Archbishop Thomas Becket, murdered in 1170.

c **St Albans Cathedral**
Built on the hill where St Alban, the first Christian martyr in England, was executed by the Romans in the third century, AD

d **Bury St Edmunds** in Suffolk. Tomb of King Edmund of East Anglia – killed by the Danes in the time of Alfred the Great.

e **Walsingham** in Norfolk, a famous statue of the Virgin Mary.

f **Durham Cathedral**
The shrine of St Cuthbert, a much loved abbot of Lindisfarne and bishop of Northumbria in the seventh century.

'Grehoundes he hadde as swift as fowel in flight;
Of prikyng (riding) and of huntyng for the hare
Was al his lust (desire), for no cost wolde he spare.'

Similarly, the friar was a worldly man who seemed to care more for pleasure than his service to God:

'He knew the tavernes wel in every toun
And everich hostiler (innkeeper) and tappestere (barmaid)
Bet than a lazar (leper) or a beggestere (beggar).'

At the time Chaucer was writing, the strict rules of St Benedict and St Francis were often ignored. Monks and friars still praised God and did good works. But they also expected to have possessions of their own, to dress smartly and enjoy sports and other worldly pleasures.

DOCUMENTS: CORRUPTION IN THE CHURCH

Document 1

The following extract is taken from an *English History* written around 1250 in the Benedictine abbey of St Albans by Matthew Paris, one of the greatest chroniclers of the Middle Ages.

An argument arose between the Franciscans and Dominicans. . . . On one side the Dominicans declared that they were established first, and were therefore more worthy; that they were also more respectably dressed, and had deservedly gained their position and reputation from their preaching . . . on the other side, the Franciscans answered that they had taken up, for God, a way of living harder and more humble, and so more worthy. . . . The Dominicans contradicted them to their face, saying that though the Franciscans went barefooted, dressed roughly and wore a rope around their waist, the privilege of eating meat or more delicate food was not denied them even in public, a thing which is forbidden to the Dominican community. . . . Therefore . . . a great and scandalous quarrel arose; and as it was between learned men and scholars, it was all the more dangerous to the Catholic Church. . . . These are the people who daily expose to view their priceless treasures, in enlarging their luxurious buildings. . . . When noblemen and men they know to possess great riches are at the point of death, they, in their love of gain, keenly urge them to make confessions and hidden wills. . . . Despising also the true orders which were established by the holy fathers, . . . they set their own community before the rest. They look upon the Cistercian monks as clownish . . . and the monks of the Black order as proud pleasure-seekers.

Adapted from Derek Baker, The Later Middle Ages, 1216–1485: Portraits and Documents, *Hutchinson, 1968, pages 113–5*

Questions

1. What seems to be Matthew Paris's purpose in reporting this dispute among the friars?
2. If you did not know that the writer belonged to the Black Monks, how would you be able to tell that he was not on the side of the friars?
3. Do you agree with Matthew Paris that this was 'a great and scandalous quarrel' and 'dangerous to the Catholic Church'? Give reasons for your views.
4. Why does the writer think the friars were so keen to help the rich make confessions and wills just before they died? What evidence is there for his suspicions?

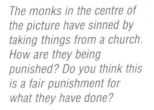

The monks in the centre of the picture have sinned by taking things from a church. How are they being punished? Do you think this is a fair punishment for what they have done?

Document 2

When bishops or archdeacons made 'visitations' to parishes ordinary parishioners called sidesmen were questioned about such things as the behaviour of the priest. The following is taken from the record of a visitation to a parish near Exeter in 1301.

St Mary Church. The parishioners say that, until the days of the present Vicar, they would maintain the Chancel in all things and be free from paying tithe for the restoration of the church; but the present Vicar, although he does not maintain the Chancel, yet receives the tithe and compels them to pay . . . they say that the Vicar feeds his beasts of all kinds in the churchyard, by whom it is evilly trodden down and vilely fouled . . . he causes his malt to be malted [beer to be brewed] in the church, wherein he stores his wheat and other goods; whereby his servants go in and out and leave the door open, and the wind blowing into the church at time of storms tends to uncover the roof. They say moreover that he preaches well and carries out all his duties in a praiseworthy fashion when he is present. But often he departs to live at Moreton-Hampstead [on Dartmoor] for a week or a fortnight.

Adapted from G. G. Coulton, Social Life in Britain, *C.U.P., 1918, pages 261–2*

Questions

1. Can you think of any reason why it is recorded that the vicar carried out all his duties well, despite the complaints against him?
2. When they speak of maintaining the church, why do the parishioners refer in particular to the chancel?
3. Why would the people of the parish be offended by the vicar brewing beer in the church and allowing his animals to feed in the churchyard?
4. It was the duty of the head of the diocese of Exeter, one Bishop Stapeldon, to discipline the vicar of St Mary Church. If you were writing a letter on his behalf, what would you say?

Document 3

The following passage has been translated into modern English from *Piers Plowman*, a long poem written by William Langland, who lived in London at the same time as Chaucer and died a few years before him. Langland's poem is in the form of a dream about the England of his day in which he is quick to point out its corruptions and abuses, especially within the Church.

I saw pilgrims . . . banding together to visit the shrines at Rome and Compostella. They went on their way full of clever talk, and took leave to tell fibs about it for the rest of their lives. . . . I saw the Friars there too . . . preaching to the people for what they could get. . . . There was also a Pardoner. . . . The ignorant folk . . . came up and knelt to kiss his documents, while he, blinding them with letters of indulgence thrust in their faces, raked in their rings and jewellery. . . .

   Bishops and . . . other great divines [important churchmen] – to whom Christ has given the charge of men's souls. . . . I saw them all living in London. . . . Some took posts at Court counting the king's money. . . . Others went into the service of lords and ladies, sitting like stewards managing household affairs – and gabbled their daily Mass . . . without devotion.

Penguin Classics, 2nd Edition, 1959, pages 63–5

Questions

1. What is Langland attacking: is it the Christian faith, clergymen, the English people, or all three?
2. What sorts of 'fibs' do you think pilgrims might have told about their visits to distant shrines? Make up one such yarn told by a pilgrim to impress friends and relations.
3. Why do you think kings and nobles were keen to get churchmen to work for them?
4. Compare Documents 3 and 4. How are Langland's and Chaucer's ways of expressing their disapproval different? Which do you find the most effective, and why?

Document 4

Of all the religious characters in Chaucer's *Canterbury Tales*, the Pardoner is the most unholy. Pardoners obtained a licence from the Pope to sell *indulgences* which let people off part of the penance or punishment that was still due after their sins had been confessed to a priest. Money collected in this way was supposed to be for the benefit of the Church, but often it found its way into pardoners' pockets. Unlike the quotations on page 121, this passage from Chaucer has been re-written into modern English.

> He'd sewed a holy relic on his cap;
> His wallet lay before him on his lap,
> Brimful of pardons come from Rome all hot.
> He had the same small voice a goat has got.
> . . . There was no pardoner of equal grace,
> For in his trunk he had a pillow-case
> Which he asserted was Our Lady's veil.
> He said he had a gobbet [fragment] of the sail
> Saint Peter had the time when he made bold
> To walk the waves, till Jesu Christ took hold.
> He had a cross of metal set with stones
> And, in a glass, a rubble of pigs' bones.
> And with these relics, any time he found
> Some poor up-country parson to astound,
> On one short day, in money down, he drew
> More than the parson in a month or two.

Penguin Classics, 1951 (translated by N. Coghill), page 38

This is an illustration from a medieval book. What is the monk doing? What does this choice of subject tell you about the artist's view of monastic life?

Questions

1. How would it benefit the Pardoner if he could convince people that he had holy relics such as Our Lady's veil?
2. What was the point of having 'a rubble of pigs' bones'?
3. Why do you think Chaucer compares the Pardoner's income with that of the parson?
4. Summarise the ways in which Chaucer expresses his obvious dislike of pardoners in this extract.

KINGS AND REBELLIOUS LORDS

MAGNA CARTA AND THE BEGINNING OF PARLIAMENT

'John, nature's enemy.'
'He plundered his own people.'
'Cruel towards all men.'
'Hell itself is fouled by the . . . presence of John.'
'No man may ever trust him.'

These are some of the things written about King John by chroniclers, during his lifetime and shortly after his death. He is often described as the worst king ever to have sat on the English throne.

Some historians now think this judgment is unfair. Certainly John had a very unpleasant side to his character. He was suspicious, untrustworthy and sometimes cruel. But as a king he had good qualities too. Like his father, Henry II, he was well educated, intelligent and very active in governing his kingdom. John was always on the move, regularly visiting every corner of the country. On his travels he saw that the laws were carried out, judged many disputes himself and kept a close watch on the work of royal officials.

In these ways John was a better ruler than his brother, Richard I. But Richard was admired for his successes on the battlefield, whereas John suffered heavy defeats. In the Middle Ages it was difficult for a king to gain respect if he failed as a warrior. In fact, John failed in most of the things he tried to do. During his reign of seventeen years (1199–1216) he was hardly ever out of trouble.

King John's troubles

John was unlucky in having to face a powerful and determined enemy – Philip II of France. It was the great ambition of Philip's

This marble effigy, or image, of King John can be seen on his tomb in Worcester Cathedral. When the tomb was opened in 1797 John was found to have been five feet five inches tall – small by modern standards, but probably about average for a man of his own day

Philip II of France

life to conquer the French lands belonging to the Plantagenet kings. Richard I had needed all his military skill to drive back Philip's armies. After the Lion-heart's death Philip, gaining in strength and confidence, continued the war against John.

The English King organised his defences with great energy, but he lacked his brother's ability to lead and inspire an army. He also harmed his cause by acts of cruelty. John's teenage nephew, Arthur, Count of Brittany, was captured while fighting against his uncle. Some months later he was murdered, almost certainly at the King's orders, and some of his followers were starved to death in prison.

Many of John's French subjects joined Philip, who soon won a string of victories. In 1204 he captured *Chateau Gaillard*, Richard I's 'unconquerable' castle, and invaded Normandy. Within two years Anjou and Brittany were also in Philip's hands. Out of all the French lands ruled by his father and brother, John was left with just Poitou and Gascony, part of the duchy of Aquitaine.

John never gave up hope of winning back his lands. But he needed money to fight another war and his attempts to get it caused trouble with the barons. As feudal lord of England, the King was entitled to certain payments from his tenants. For example, when a baron died his son had to pay what was called a *relief* before he could take over his father's estate. John often demanded much larger reliefs than previous kings had done. The same hap-

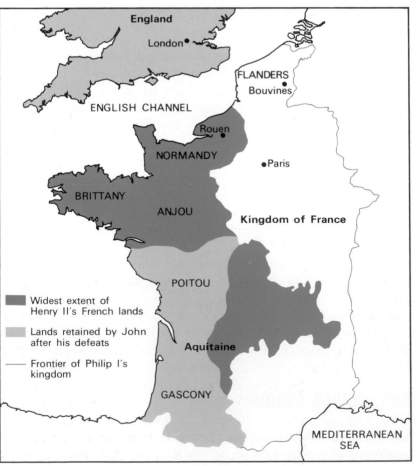

France in the reign of John. He lost more than two-thirds of his French lands to Philip II

pened with *scutage* – the payment kings could claim instead of military service. John asked for larger scutages, and claimed them more frequently. In all he collected as many scutages (eleven) as Henry II and Richard I put together, and in less than half the time.

There was a good reason for John's greater demands. Prices were rising rapidly during his reign. It cost him up to 24 pence a day to hire one knight, whereas his father had paid only eightpence. Opposition to John grew as the money seemed to produce few results and because he tried to bully many baronial families. The barons accused the King of going against the 'customs of the realm'. There were no laws fixing limits to feudal payments, but each king was expected to follow the practice of previous rulers.

John also got into trouble with the Church. In 1206 he quarrelled with the Pope, Innocent III, who refused to accept his choice of a new archbishop of Canterbury. After much disagreement Innocent selected Stephen Langton, an Englishman living in his court in Rome. Stephen was a good choice, but John rejected him, claiming it was usual for kings to have a say in these appointments. He was right. No English king since the Conquest had failed to get an archbishop he wanted.

Innocent would not give way. In 1208 he put England under an *interdict*, which meant all churches were locked and no services held except baptism of infants and confession for the dying. There were no marriages and no one could be buried in holy ground. This caused great distress at a time when religion was the most powerful force in people's lives. But John seemed in no hurry to settle the dispute. He seized the lands of several monasteries and forced a number of clergymen supporting the Pope to leave England. Innocent's reply was to *excommunicate* the King (expel him from the Church).

Not until 1213 did John give in and accept Langton, who ended the excommunication. The interdict was lifted the following year, and all over the kingdom people rejoiced to hear again the peal of church bells. John's quarrel with the Pope partly explains the nasty things written about him at the time. He did not, in fact, hate the Church. But monks, who wrote most of the chronicles, believed that a king who was excommunicated must be an evil monster.

The seal of Archbishop Stephen Langton

Baronial rebellion

John made a determined effort to recover his French lands in the summer of 1214. On his side was the German Emperor, Otto IV, who agreed to attack King Philip from the north while John came up from the south. But Philip defeated Otto at Bouvines, in Flanders, and the plan was ruined. John returned to England, short of money, to face a baronial rebellion.

A powerful group of barons had been plotting against John for some time. Many had been forced to pay vast sums of money to the King, and some had been denied proper justice in his court. The time had come for a showdown. If John had been victorious in France he could have stood up to them. But when he failed again he lost the support of a number of barons who had previously been faithful.

Hoping to prevent bloodshed, Archbishop Stephen Langton got the rebels to draw up a list of grievances and present them to the King. These accused him of ignoring certain customs established by past kings and demanded that he must make a solemn promise to keep to them in future. John was furious! Never before had an English king been expected to obey written rules, and he had no intention of being the first to do so. When their demands were rejected, the barons decided to use force. In April 1215 they gathered their armed knights at Stamford in Lincolnshire and began marching south.

John still had some support. Most of the sheriffs remained loyal. So did his *constables* (in charge of the royal castles) and a few of the greatest barons – including William Marshal, Earl of Pembroke, one of the most respected men in England. Nevertheless John could not prevent the rebels from occupying London. He fled to Windsor Castle and asked for peace, knowing it was useless to resist any longer. On 15 June the two sides met in a meadow called Runnymede, beside the River Thames between Staines and Windsor.

The Great Charter

Discussions went on for several days at Runnymede before the terms of peace were agreed. Then everything that the King had promised was written in Latin on a piece of parchment, and a wax impression of the Great Seal was attached to it. This document, one of the most important in all English history, became known as *Magna Carta* (Latin for 'the Great Charter').

Many copies of the Great Charter were made by royal clerks in the summer of 1215. They were sent to sheriffs and other important officials, so that all leading subjects could be told what the King had granted. Only four of these copies exist today – one in Lincoln Cathedral, one in Salisbury Cathedral and two in the British Museum.

Magna Carta was granted to all freemen of England. But the barons gained most from it. They aimed to make John rule according to the 'customs of the realm'. So they got him to set out in the Charter what they believed these customs to be.

In future John was not to ask for scutage until his tenants-in-chief had agreed to it. And the relief a baron had to pay when he inherited his father's lands was fixed at £100 (some had paid several thousand pounds earlier in John's reign). Knights also benefited from the Charter, because it said barons must grant to their own tenants what the King was granting them. The relief of a knight was fixed at £5 – the usual amount in Henry II's time.

Next to regulations about money payments the most important parts of Magna Carta were to do with justice. John had considered the giving of justice to be a personal favour which he could refuse if he wanted to. He made some unfortunate barons pay large sums

One side of John's Great Seal, showing him sitting on his throne. Every copy of Magna Carta *carried a wax impression of this seal, which measures 9 centimetres across. Such documents were sealed to show they were genuine. Nowadays we simply write our signature*

One of the two copies of Magna Carta in the British Museum, London. (The other was damaged by fire in 1731.) This copy measures 51 centimetres by 34, and probably took a clerk the best part of a day to write out. Such charters did not have paragraphs, but it is usual to divide Magna Carta into sixty-three short sections

of money just to get a fair trial. In future, no freeman was to be punished without a proper trial and the King was not to sell or deny justice to anyone.

The Charter granted many more baronial demands. For example, the royal forests were to be reduced in size, certain unpopular sheriffs and foreign judges were to be dismissed, and the English Church was to be free to obey the Pope. A committee of twenty-five barons was chosen to keep a check on the King. They were ready to use force if he broke his promises. But although the Charter allowed this committee to be formed John had no intention of taking orders from it. He preferred to fight rather than allow barons to sit in judgment on him. So in September 1215 civil war broke out again.

With borrowed money, John hired soldiers from the Continent and put up a strong resistance. But he did not live to see the end of the fighting. In the night of 18 October 1216, he died suddenly at Newark in Nottinghamshire, after heavy eating and drinking. 'At his end', wrote a chronicler, 'few mourned for him.' However, John's death did not mean Magna Carta was forgotten. It became part of the law of the land and in the years ahead barons made sure kings remembered what it said.

Earl Simon's Parliament

John's nine-year old son was crowned King Henry III, and a group of loyal barons began to govern the country until the boy was old enough to rule. The civil war soon ended and a new

Bronze figure of Henry III in Westminster Abbey

version of Magna Carta was issued which included most of the things granted by John. For a while the barons seemed satisfied and the kingdom was at peace.

Henry grew up into a kind and gentle man. He had a good education and loved books, painting and architecture. But although he was more pleasant than his father he lacked strength and firmness. He allowed his French wife, Eleanor, to crowd his court with her friends and relations. Many of these foreigners were given large estates and important positions in the King's government. Henry even allowed the Pope to appoint about 300 foreign clergymen to English churches.

The English barons and Church leaders complained bitterly. They were supposed to be the King's advisers, yet he took little notice of them, preferring to listen to his foreign courtiers. In 1258 the English barons finally lost patience. They met at Oxford and demanded changes in the way the country was being governed. Henry was forced to hand over most of his power to a council of fifteen barons, led by Simon de Montfort, Earl of Leicester.

Unfortunately the barons soon began to argue amongst themselves. Some were jealous of Earl Simon's power and encouraged Henry to oppose the council of fifteen. 'Servants should not judge their masters', said the King. But when he raised an army to punish the rebels he was defeated and taken prisoner (1264).

For a while Simon de Montfort was practically the ruler of England. He assembled Great Councils just as though he were a king. But many nobles refused to co-operate with him. So to gain wider support Simon tried an experiment in January 1265 which was to have important consequences for the future. He held a Great Council to which he invited not only the nobles who supported him but also the representatives of ordinary freemen. Each county was asked to send two knights, and each town that was friendly to him sent two *burgesses* (citizens).

Simon de Montfort, from a window in Chartres Cathedral in France

Never before had tenants-in-chief been joined by both knights and townsmen to discuss the government of the realm. But if it was the first time it was certainly not the last. This sort of assembly later came to be called a *Parliament*. Simon's main support was among the knights and burgesses – that is why he invited them. But their presence was also a sign of the growing influence of lesser landowners and town merchants in the affairs of the kingdom.

King, Lords and Commons

The rule of Simon de Montfort came to a sudden end in the summer of 1265. Many of his followers changed sides and he was defeated by Prince Edward, the King's eldest son, in a bloody battle at Evesham in Worcestershire. Outnumbered and penned in against the banks of the River Avon, all the rebel leaders were slaughtered. Simon's dead body was cut into pieces by a knight who had earlier supported him. The chronicler Matthew Paris mourned his death:

Thus ended the labours of that noble man Earl Simon, who

gave up not only his property, but also his person . . . for the maintenance of justice and the rights of the kingdom. . . .
Report goes that Simon, after his death, was distinguished by the working of many miracles, which, however, were not made publicly known, for fear of kings.

Prince Edward, strong and vigorous, took over from his ageing father and promised to rule according to Magna Carta. Seven years later Henry died and Edward became king in his own right (1272–1307). Although he had restored the power of the Crown, Edward I set out to rule with the help and agreement of his subjects. He took up Simon de Montfort's idea and from time to time (beginning in 1275) he invited knights and burgesses to attend his Great Council of nobles. He listened to their complaints and asked them to agree, in the name of the people, to the collection of certain taxes.

Such gatherings gave the King and his subjects a chance to *parley* (talk) and this is how we get the word Parliament. Meetings of Parliament could take place anywhere, but they were usually held in the hall of the royal palace at Westminster. The modern Houses of Parliament stand on the same site.

In Edward's reign, and for a long time afterwards, the barons and bishops of the Great Council (known as 'the Lords') were the most powerful members of Parliament. The knights and burgesses ('the Commons') were only invited on special occasions at first. But their control of taxation made them increasingly important. In time, two separate Houses of Parliament developed – Lords and Commons.

As well as agreeing to taxation, the Commons presented *petitions* (requests) to the King. If he agreed to a petition he wrote on it, in French, 'le roi le veult' (the king wills it) and it became law. Such petitions were the first Parliamentary Bills. When a Bill becomes law nowadays the monarch's approval is still written in French.

In the Middle Ages Parliament only met when it was called by the King. Its task was to give advice, not make decisions on its own. There were no political parties, and no one thought of asking peasants or other lesser folk to elect members to represent them in Parliament. Only people with property were thought fit to take part in governing. Not until quite recent times did Parliament take the form it has today.

Timeline

AD
1199–1216	Reign of John
1204	Loss of Normandy to Philip II
1208–14	England under an interdict
1215	Magna Carta
1216–72	Reign of Henry III
1258	Baronial rebellion
1265	Simon de Montfort's Parliament – and death
1272–1307	Reign of Edward I

In the image: *Xlexander Rex Scotoz* — *lewellin princeps vocatt*

Parliament in the days of Edward I, showing the King with his tenants-in-chief, and his Treasurer, Chancellor and other royal officials. Llewellyn, Prince of Wales, and King Alexander of Scotland are also present on this occasion. The 'Commons', if they were invited, did not sit with the Great Council. After a brief speech by the Chancellor they left the main hall to discuss the King's proposals among themselves

Sources and questions

1. Look at the picture above.
   (a) Where is Edward I? What makes it easy to identify him?
   (b) Apart from the visitors from Scotland and Wales, can you find anyone else dressed like royalty? Who might it be?
   (c) How can you identify the clerks who are writing a record of what is said?
   (d) Can you pick out the bishops? Two of them are made to look more important than the others. Do you know why?

(e) What other sorts of people were at this meeting of the King's Great Council? Can you describe them in the picture?

2. Write or act out an imaginary conversation between King John and Archbishop Stephen Langton at Runnymede. (The Archbishop is trying to persuade John to agree to the barons' demands, but the King is angry and very stubborn.)

3. John was Henry II's favourite son, and his father would have preferred to see him rule ahead of Richard.

   If Henry had come back to life after 1216, what do you think he would have said about the reigns of his sons? Would he have changed his preference for John? Give reasons for your views.

4. Here is another extract from the chronicles of Matthew Paris. Writing in the early 1250s, he is expressing his disapproval of one of King Henry III's foreign favourites.

   The King . . . continued to distribute vacant estates and their incomes amongst . . . undeserving foreigners. . . .
   We think it right to mention here the following case, as one out of many. In the service of Geoffrey de Lusignan, the King's brother, was a certain chaplain, who served as a fool and jester to the King, to the said Geoffrey his master and all the court, and whose sayings . . . contributed to their amusement and made them laugh; and on this man the King bestowed the rich church of Preston. . . . This same chaplain, a Poitevin by birth [from Poitou in central France], utterly ignorant in both manners and learning, we have seen pelting the King, his brother Geoffrey and other nobles, whilst walking in the orchard of St Albans, with turf, stones and green apples, and pressing the juice of unripe grapes in their eyes, like one lacking in sense. His gestures, way of speaking and habits are equally despicable, as in his size and personal appearance. This man seems more like a stage actor than a priest, to the great disgrace of the priestly order. Such are the persons to whom the King of England entrusts the care and protection of many thousands of souls, rejecting such a vast number of educated, wise and proper men born in England.

   Adapted from Derek Baker, The Later Middle Ages, 1216–1485, *Hutchinson, 1968, pages 4–5*

(a) How does this document help to explain why there was a rebellion against Henry III a few years later?
(b) List all the writer's reasons for disapproving of the chaplain. Do you find any of his criticisms unfair?
(c) Why do you think Matthew Paris feels so strongly about such matters – even to the extent of criticising his King?
(d) How does this document help us to understand better the quotation from the same writer on pages 150–51?

EDWARD I, WALES AND SCOTLAND

Coin showing Edward I – known as 'Longshanks' because he was very tall. When his tomb in Westminster Abbey was opened, the embalmed body was found to measure 6 feet 2 inches – an enormous size for a man of the thirteenth century. A wise and firm ruler, who cared for order and justice, Edward was also an outstanding soldier and more religious than most medieval kings

When the English invaded Britain, back in the fifth and sixth centuries, their advances was halted at the uplands of the North and West. The Scottish and Welsh hill folk grew up as separate peoples, sharing the mainland of Britain with the English. The Irish too, separated by sea, kept their own rulers, language and traditions.

In later centuries armies from England tried to conquer the outlying parts of the British Isles. They had little success in Ireland. Henry II invaded its eastern shores in 1171 but his efforts were not followed up. By the end of the Middle Ages only Dublin and the surrounding area remained under the rule of the English Crown. However, Wales and Scotland, unprotected by sea, faced frequent attacks from the neighbouring English.

It was in the reign of Edward I (1272–1307) that the English made their greatest assault on Welsh and Scottish freedom. 'Warlike as a leopard, Edward shines out like a new Richard', wrote one of his subjects. But unlike Richard I, who fought mostly in France, Edward tried to master the mainland of Britain.

Llewellyn, Lord of Snowdonia

The Welsh were a warlike people, living in a rugged, mountainous land. There were very few areas flat enough to be ploughed and sown with crops. In these parts – near the coast, along river valleys and on the Isle of Anglesey – farmers settled in villages. But up in the hills scattered tribes of herdsmen lived with their cattle, sheep and goats. As they wandered from place to place in search of fresh pastures, these wild, restless folk constantly fought each other. Brave deeds in war were remembered in the ballads of minstrels, called *bards*, who sang in the halls of tribal chiefs.

King Offa's dyke (see page 65) kept the Welsh and English apart in Saxon times, except for border raids by cattle rustlers. But the Norman Conquest of England brought changes. To guard the border country, known as the *Welsh Marches*, William I gave large estates to the earls of Chester, Shrewsbury and Hereford. These 'marcher lords' and their descendants began to advance

Wales in the time of Edward I

across the frontier into central and southern Wales. But in the mountainous North-West, topped by the peak of Snowdon, the Welsh chiefs were still free and determined to fight back.

When Edward I became king, Snowdonia – or *Gwynedd* as the Welsh called it – was ruled by a powerful chief named Llewellyn. He had recently re-conquered most of central Wales from the marcher lords and forced all the lesser Welsh chiefs to obey him. Now there were signs that Llewellyn had still greater ambitions. In a treaty made with Edward's father, Henry III, Llewellyn had agreed to pay homage to the English King as his overlord. But when Edward came to the throne the Lord of Snowdonia missed the coronation ceremony and proudly refused to renew his homage.

After several reminders had brought excuses from Llewellyn, Edward declared war. In 1277 he led an army along the north coast of Wales, while the marcher lords advanced further south. Llewellyn retired to the safety of the mountains. But he was soon starved into surrender when Edward's ships cut off corn supplies from Anglesey. The King treated Llewellyn fairly. Once he had paid homage he was left in control of Gwynedd, but he had to give up his other lands.

There matters might have rested, but for Llewellyn's brother David. Complaining at the harsh treatment of his countrymen by English officials, David rebelled in the spring of 1282. Llewellyn joined him, reluctantly, and all Wales rose in revolt. The King now decided to crush the troublesome Welsh once and for all. Again Llewellyn was surrounded by the English in his mountain stronghold. This time he broke free and escaped southwards, but he was killed in a skirmish at Orewin Bridge, near Builth, in December 1282.

Beaumaris Castle on the Isle of Anglesey. It was begun in 1295, after a Welsh revolt the previous year. No less than 400 stonemasons were employed in constructing it. Notice the outer ring wall completely surrounds the defences inside.

Llewellyn's head was sent in triumph to London and fixed on a spear above the Tower. Six months later David was captured and executed. By then Welsh resistance had already collapsed. Edward took control of Snowdonia and divided it into counties, like the rest of his kingdom. The marcher lords were given lands in Wales, which was now wholly under English law and government. The Welsh were no longer independent, but to this day they have kept alive their Celtic language and many old customs.

Castles among the conquered

To strengthen his hold on Wales, Edward built castles round the fringes of Snowdonia. Without delay the work of construction began at Conway, Caernarvon and Harlech. A further castle, at Beaumaris on Anglesey, was started a few years later. All four were situated near the coast, so their garrisons of English soldiers could receive supplies by sea if the Welsh rose in revolt.

Edward had built other castles in Wales earlier in his reign (see map). But they could not compare with the mighty fortresses round Snowdonia, which are among the finest of the Middle Ages. Instead of having a single square keep, like earlier stone castles, Edward's architects planned *concentric* defences (one circle of walls inside another). The most important rooms led into a central quadrangle, or *inner ward*. Beyond this, between the two rings of walls, was the narrow *outer ward*. Here any attackers who got past the main gate would be caught between two showers of arrows.

The towers built into the walls were important for defence. In the old square keeps it was impossible for archers to shoot at attackers close underneath the walls without exposing themselves to returning fire. But in these later castles towers curving outwards made it easy for defenders inside to shoot along the faces of the walls.

Edward I's great Welsh castles still stand today as monuments to his reign. It was at Caernarvon that his son, the future Edward II, was born in 1284 – most probably in temporary royal quarters on the site of the present castle. When the young Edward was seventeen his father gave him the title Prince of Wales. Ever since then monarchs' eldest sons have received the same honour.

Llewellyn's death almost marks the end of the long struggle between the Welsh and the English – but not quite. A century later, in 1400, a powerful Welsh landowner, Owen Glendower, led his people in a last bid for freedom. Many castles of King Henry IV and his marcher lords were captured by the rebels, and a number of English armies were defeated. At the height of his power Owen controlled nearly the whole of Wales. But after several years of bloodshed and destruction the fires of revolt flickered out. Owen disappeared and died in an unknown hiding place.

'The Hammer of the Scots'

Unlike Wales, Scotland had its own line of kings. They ruled over a country which fell into two distinct halves. In the rolling hills and lowlands south of the Firth of Forth there lived many families of English and Norman descent. Here land was shared out among feudal lords and the way of life was similar to that in England.

The castle and town walls of Conway. The whole circuit is 1280 metres round, with three gates and twenty-one towers

Stirling Castle today. Most of the medieval buildings have been replaced, but the picture shows the excellent defensive position of the castle, known as 'the Gateway to the Highlands'

Effigy of Edward II, from his tomb in Gloucester Cathedral. Although athletic and courageous, he was not the warrior king that the English nobles looked for. He preferred music and play-acting to fighting. He was deposed and murdered by his own nobles in 1327

in a cave, watching a spider try to make its web. After many falls it finally succeeded and Bruce gained fresh heart. The story may well have been invented, but Bruce's recovery was real enough. One by one he captured the English-held castles, until after seven years Stirling, the greatest of them all, was at his mercy.

Edward II could not let Stirling fall without a fight. In June 1314 he crossed the Border with about 20,000 men. Bruce's army was outnumbered by three to one, but it was well placed, on a wooded ridge above a stream called the Bannock Burn, just south of Stirling. The two armies met on Midsummer's Day, the Scots attacking downhill and taking the enemy by surprise. The fighting was long and bitter, but the Scots were better led and more confident. After suffering heavy losses, the English fled in disorder.

The battle of Bannockburn was the greatest blow ever struck for Scottish freedom. In 1328 a new English king, Edward III, finally made peace with Bruce and accepted him as the rightful ruler of Scotland. Edward I's plan to unite the English and Scottish crowns had to wait another 300 years, until 1603, when James VI of Scotland became James I of a United Kingdom. In the meantime, both countries went on quarrelling and fighting.

Statue of Robert Bruce (1274–1329) at Stirling Castle

Timeline

AD

1272–1307	Reign of Edward I
1277	Edward I's first Welsh campaign
1282	Welsh rebellion crushed; death of Llewellyn
1296	Edward I's first Scottish campaign
1298	Battle of Falkirk; Edward I master of Scotland
1306	Robert Bruce crowned King of Scotland
1314	Edward II defeated at battle of Bannockburn

DOCUMENTS: TROUBLESOME WELSH AND SCOTS

Document 1

This is taken from a letter written by Llewellyn, the prince of Wales, to King Edward I in July 1273.

> We have received the letter written in the king's name, dated Westminster 20 June, forbidding us to construct a castle on our own land near Aber Miwl, or to establish a town or market there. We are sure that the letter was not issued with your knowledge . . . for you know well that the rights of our principality are entirely separate from the rights of your kingdom, although we hold our principality under your royal power. You have heard and in part seen that we and our ancestors had the power within our boundaries to build castles and forts and create markets without prohibition by anyone or any announcement of new work. We pray you not to listen to the evil suggestions of those who seek to poison your mind against us.

Quoted in F. M. Powicke, Henry III and the Lord Edward, *O.U.P., 1947, pages 621–2*

Questions

1. What is Llewellyn's attitude to the English King, as revealed by his letter?
2. Before Edward's succession to the throne the previous year, what events would have increased Llewellyn's confidence and sense of importance?
3. Why do you think the king's tenants-in-chief had to seek royal permission to do any of the things referred to in the letter? Why would Edward not want to treat Llewellyn differently?
4. What do you think Llewellyn hoped to achieve by writing in this way?

The gateway of Harlech Castle, built by Edward I. Nowadays visitors pass between the empty towers by means of a solid bridge, and steps. Can you describe what this gateway would have been like in Edward's day, from an attacker's point of view?

Document 2

The writer of the following extract, Lodewyk van Veltham, lived in Flanders (what is now Belgium). He was able to observe the habits of these Welshmen at their camp while they were fighting in the army of Edward I during a military campaign on the Continent in 1297.

> There you saw the peculiar habits of the Welsh. In the very depth of winter they were running about bare-legged. They wore a red robe. They could not have been warm. The money they received from the king was spent in milk and butter. They would eat and drink anywhere. I never saw them wearing armour. I studied them very closely and walked among them to find out what defensive armour they carried when going into battle. Their weapons were bows, arrows and swords . . . They wore linen clothing. They were great drinkers. . . . Their pay was too small and so it came about that they took what did not belong to them.

Quoted in F. M. Powicke, The Thirteenth Century, *O.U.P., 1953, page 384*

Questions

1. Why was the writer's attention drawn to these Welsh troops? How might they have differed from others in the King's army?
2. Why might Edward I have been keen to put Welshmen in his army at this time?
3. Are the facts in this account likely to be correct? Give your reasons.
4. What do you think are the writer's feelings about these Welshmen?

This picture of peasants ploughing is one of many illustrations in a book of psalms (The Luttrell Psalter) dating from about 1340. The plough was mostly made of wood, but its cutting parts (the coulter and share) were made of iron. The large part by the ploughman's foot is the mould-board. It pushes the soil sideways and helps to make the furrow

So groups of villagers worked together, each contributing a share in the ploughing team. Eight oxen might be needed altogether, although teams of four or two could be used on lighter soils.

When the land had been ploughed corn crops were sown – perhaps wheat or rye in one field in the autumn, and barley in another in the spring. The third field remained *fallow* (unsown after ploughing) so that the soil could recover its richness. The fallow period came to each field in rotation, one year out of three. There were no artificial fertilisers in the Middle Ages. If corn was sown on the same land every year the soil got poorer and poorer.

As well as their strips, villeins had small patches of land round their huts. Here they grew peas, beans, leeks, onions and other vegetables. Perhaps they had fruit trees too, providing apples, pears or cherries in season. Some of the poorest peasants, called *bordars* or *cottars*, had no strips in the fields and so depended on their 'cottage gardens'. However, the lord usually hired them for money when extra hands were needed.

Sowing the crops. The peasants normally had seeds in baskets or bags. They broadcast (scattered) them by hand into the furrows

Cutting hay with a long curved scythe. Dry weather was essential, otherwise the hay might be spoilt. Hence the saying 'make hay while the sun shines'

Harvesting the corn with a sickle. This is smaller than a scythe and has a crescent-shaped blade. When the corn was cut it was tied into sheaves and taken to the barns

Threshing (beating) the corn, to get the grains out of their husks. It was done with jointed sticks called flails. Sacks of grain were then taken to the miller to be ground into flour

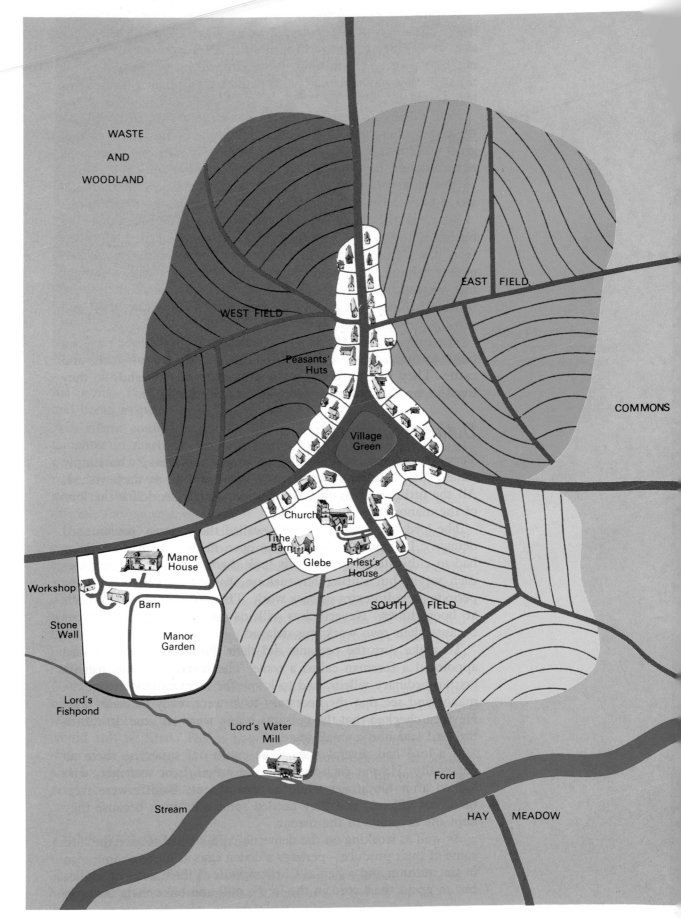

WASTE

AND

WOODLAND

EAST FIELD

WEST FIELD

Peasants' Huts

COMMONS

Village Green

Church

Tithe Barn

Glebe

Priest's House

Manor House

Workshop

Barn

Stone Wall

Manor Garden

SOUTH FIELD

Lord's Fishpond

Lord's Water Mill

Ford

Stream

HAY MEADOW

Plan of an 'open field' village. Strips were usually marked out with lines of wooden pegs or stones. The size of the three fields was not fixed; as the village population grew, more land was brought into cultivation. There were no proper roads, only rough tracks or paths moat. Like castles, manor houses often had cellars on the ground floor and the main room, or hall, on the first floor. In the hall meals were served, and at other times women of the household did their spinning and embroidery, children played, and the lord gave orders to his servants. The manor court was often held in the hall, and every night servants slept there, on benches or on the rushes covering the oak floor.

Early manor houses had a fireplace in the middle of the hall. The smoke escaped through an opening in the roof. In later years a fireplace and chimney were built into one of the walls. But even with a roaring fire the hall was cold and draughty in winter. One way of reducing draughts was to hang tapestries on the walls. Another was to build a wooden screen inside the main entrance to the hall. Doors were cut in the screen and often a minstrels' galley was built above it.

Next to the hall was a private room called the *bower*, where guests were received. Here the lord, his lady and their younger children also slept. The lord's bed had curtains round it to keep out draughts. Clothes were kept in heavy wooden chests, but there were no upholstered chairs and carpets were rare. The kitchen was well away from the living quarters, because of the fire-risk. Next to it was the pantry, large enough to hold whole carcasses of meat, and a *buttery* ('bottlery') where wine and ale were stored.

Fruit trees, vegetables and flowers grew in the garden. The lady of the manor also planted herbs, which she used to make medicines for the sick people of the village. Nearby, there was a fish-pond and various farm buildings, including a barn, cattle-shed and stables. As time went by manor houses were enlarged, with extra bedrooms, cellars and a chapel. If the lord was very wealthy he might have glass windows put in. But glass was a great extravagance, normally used only in large churches and the richest homes.

A water mill. The wheel turns two great grindstones inside, and these grind the grains of corn into flour. Some villages had a windmill instead, but these were uncommon. In fact windmills were unknown in England before the late twelfth century

help their parents.
looked after the fa
Sundays and summ
and made swings
the village green
wedding, 'bride a
excuse for heavy c
such gatherings we

Throughout the
was a special time
1 May two young
and crowned with
round a maypole.
had a feast round a
a leg of mutton o
when the hay-cutt
into the meadow.

Other festivals
get the word 'holi
everyone went to r
in the calendar. N
fifteen to twenty
such as Christmas

Before Christm
woods, and holly,
lords gave a Chris
February came th
until Easter. On S
any remaining egg
Sunday arrived c
church was decora

Sources and

1. Look at the
   (a) What ani
   Does the use
   nature of the
   (b) What is t
   doing? Why i
   (c) The horse
   set with iron
   point of this?
   (d) On the le
   do you think
   ordinary villa

2. The following
   life and work
   thirteen cei

The remains of Stokesay 'Castle' – a manor house in Shropshire. Notice the stone keep, built in case of attack. This really makes it a cross between a castle and a house

Eating in the hall

The lord and his household usually got up at dawn. After a breakfast of bread, meat and ale, both lord and lady were kept busy giving instructions to the servants. Then, if the weather was fine, the lord and his bailiff might ride round the manor, to see that all was in order. His children, meanwhile, had lessons in Latin and French, sometimes from the village parson.

Everyone was hungry and ready for dinner before midday. The lord and older members of his family sat at the 'high table'. This stood across the end of the hall, on a low platform, or *dais*. Servants, young children and others of lower rank sat on benches at trestle tables, put up lengthwise down the hall. At each place the butler laid spoons, knives, drinking cups and bread rolls. Salt cellars were also put out.

There were no table forks. Most eating was done with the fingers, so pages carried round jugs of water and napkins. After a bowl of vegetable soup the main course was served. It might consist of boiled beef or mutton, roast pork, or perhaps bream or

A lord's high table. Instead of plates, slices of stale bread called trenchers were put out. These were collected up after the meal and given to the poor. Today, when a wealthy man gives away something he has no use for we speak of 'crumbs from the rich man's table'

A Norman manor house at Boothby Pagnell in Lincolnshire. Notice the steps leading up to the first floor, and the rounded arches over the door and most of the windows. The large square window was put in later. Early manor houses were dark inside because, without glass, windows had to be very small (to reduce draughts)

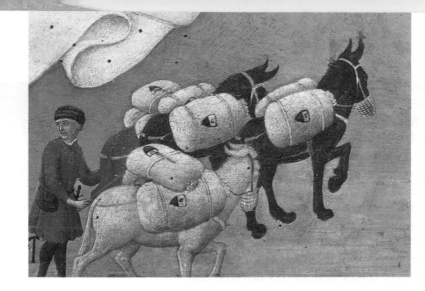

Packhorses carrying woolpacks. Most merchants used packhorses because few roads were fit for carts or wagons. For several months of the year thick mud and deep ruts made many roads and tracks impassable

'Spinsters' at work. The girl in the middle uses the things like hair brushes to 'card' or disentangle the wool. The one on the left holds a distaff under her arm (a stick with prongs to hold the mass of wool). The yarn is drawn out and twisted by a spindle (a kind of heavy spinning top)

roach, boiled
Fridays, as rul
sometimes a s
custard. Ale w

The second
food was simil
important gues
Then silver g
wine. Venison
was served – p

When darkn
flaming torche
acrobat or jest
the gallery min
ballads. After
men to their d
snapped up bo

Pastimes a

The lord spen
If there were
hares would be
and terriers. F
falconer traine
heads. At the
able prey the

When their
that are still p
ropes. On a s
and chess. Bo
with bows an
singing and da
so they had a
to-do families.

Peasant chi

The queen from a chess set used in the Middle Ages. It was probably made of walrus-tusk, in Scotland

A woman weaving on a hand-loom. This was usually men's work. To make the best broadcloth a wider 'broadloom' was used, which needed two men to work it

Dyers at work. Notice the bundle of sticks, used to feed the fire under the vat. Common dyes, such as woad (blue and black), madder (red) and weld (yellow) were made from plants grown in England. But others, including saffron (a yellow made from crocuses) and scarlet (made from an insect found in the Mediterranean lands) had to be imported although spinning wheels were also used in the later Middle Ages. Spinning was young women's work – hence the term 'spinster' for one who is unmarried. Next the yarn was woven on a loom, worked by hand and foot. It could be dyed either before or after weaving.

There now followed an important process called fulling. The cloth was beaten in water to shrink and thicken it and give it a felted look. This could be done with clubs or with feet and hands. From the twelfth century, fulling mills were introduced – simple water-mills which turned wooden hammers attached to a revolving drum. These speeded up fulling and made it more effective. Finally, the cloth was stretched out to dry and its surface brushed and levelled with a pair of shears.

As a rule each group of craftsmen worked at home, in their own workshops. A merchant 'clothier' bought the wool and passed it on from one group of craftsmen to the next. He paid them for their work and then sold the finished product himself. We call this 'domestic industry', in contrast to modern factory industry in which workers are gathered in one place.

By the fifteenth century English cloth-makers were outpacing their rivals in Flanders and Italy. The main centre of the industry was now in the Cotswold Hills, where fast flowing streams drove the fulling mills. All over Europe high prices were paid for 'broadcloths' from Castle Combe, Stroud, Bradford-on-Avon, Cirencester and other thriving villages and small towns. Instead of being exported, England's wool was used by her own craftsmen. England became as famous for finished cloth as it had once been for raw wool.

Trade over the seas

At this moment vast quantities of goods are being shipped to and from England safely and speedily. But in the Middle Ages sea

Model of a fifteenth century cog. Sailors today would not think such ships fit for more than coastal trading. But in medieval times they battled across the Baltic and North Seas. There were no warships in northern Europe, so merchant vessels had to be used in sea battles. Hence the 'castles' at each end, used by archers. We still call a raised deck at the front of a ship the fo'c'sle (forecastle)

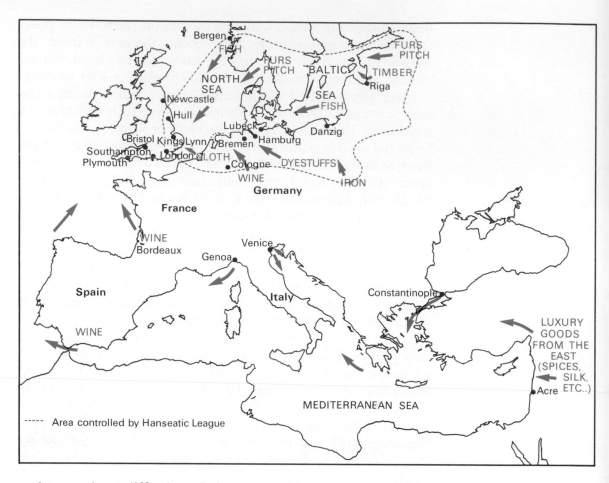

English imports in the later Middle Ages

trade was slow, difficult and dangerous. Maps were unreliable, pirates thick along many coasts and the ships themselves unsafe in rough seas. The merchants of northern Europe carried their cargoes in short, blunt-ended sailing vessels called *cogs*. These had rudders at the stern, like modern ships, but few had more than one mast and their square sails made progress against the wind very difficult.

Most trade between England and the Continent was controlled by powerful groups or companies of foreign merchants. The largest of these – the *Hanseatic League* – was formed in the twelfth century by trading towns near the Baltic and North Sea coasts. Hanse merchants, mostly Germans, set up a base in London with the permission of Henry III. Their ships brought salted fish, timber, dyestuffs, furs, pitch and iron goods. In return they bought English goods for re-sale on the Continent. Apart from London, other east coast ports, including Newcastle, Hull and King's Lynn, profited from trading with the Hanse merchants.

The Hanseatic League controlled most of the trade of northern Europe. Similarly, Italian merchants from Venice and Genoa dominated trade with the Mediterranean lands and the countries of the East. Their long, graceful galleys were frequent visitors to Bristol, Plymouth, Southampton and especially London. Italians brought mainly luxury goods – silks and other rare fabrics, carpets, jewels, ivory, gold, perfume, glassware, Mediterranean fruits and wines, and above all spices such as pepper, ginger, nutmeg and cloves.

The Italian merchants, skilled at banking and book-keeping, became the most powerful group of foreign traders in London. To this day the chief banking district in the City is Lombard Street (named after the Lombards of North Italy). Londoners were jealous of the Lombards' wealth and blamed them for every misfortune that befell the City. Occasionally there were riots against foreigners – not only Italians but also Hanse and other merchants.

To pay for imports, the English exported mainly food and raw materials – wool, corn, hides, cheese, tin from Cornwall, and lead from Derbyshire. But in the later Middle Ages the growth of industries, especially cloth-making, meant manufactured goods could be sold too. Besides woollen cloth, England exported fine leather goods and cups, mugs and plates made from pewter (a mixture of lead and tin). English merchants also began to take a hand in the export trade. Groups of *Merchant Adventurers* were formed in the main ports, with the aim of founding trading centres abroad, as their rivals had done in England. The Merchant Adventurers were to play a great part in the future growth of English trade.

London's Lombard Street today – named after the medieval Italian merchants who inhabited this part of the city

DOCUMENTS: TOWNS AND TOWN DWELLERS

Document 1

This is part of a description of London in the late twelfth century. It comes from a biography of Thomas Becket written by William fitz Stephen, one of Henry II's sheriffs and travelling judges.

On the east stands the Palatine castle [Tower of London], very big and strong. . . . On the west stand two strongly fortified castles, from which runs a continuous massive and high wall, with seven double gates and with towers at intervals along the north sides. . . . On the north there are pastures and pleasant meadows through which flow streams which turn cheerful-sounding mill-wheels. Near at hand there is an extensive forest with woodland grazing and the lairs of wild animals, red and fallow deer, wild boars and bulls. . . . Also in the northern outskirts of London are excellent wells, with sweet, clear drinking water that ripples over the bright stones. . . . These are visited by . . . crowds . . . seeking fresh air on summer evenings. . . . Immediately outside one of the gates is a field which is smooth both in fact and in name [Smithfield]. Every sixth day of the week . . . there takes place there a well-attended show of splendid horses for sale. To it come all the earls, barons and knights. . . .

Adapted from J. J. Bagley, Historical Interpretation, *Penguin, 1965, pages 78–9*

Questions

1. Write down words and phrases in the passage which show the author's liking for the City.
2. How might this be a flattering picture of London? (Document 2 contains some clues, even though it refers to English towns 200 years later.)
3. Can you explain why the City's defences seem to be concentrated in the east, west and north?
4. Why would earls, barons and knights have been especially interested in the horse sales?
5. Imagine you are living in the London of William fitz Stephen and writing to invite a friend to come and stay with you. Tell your friend about some of the things you will be able to do together.

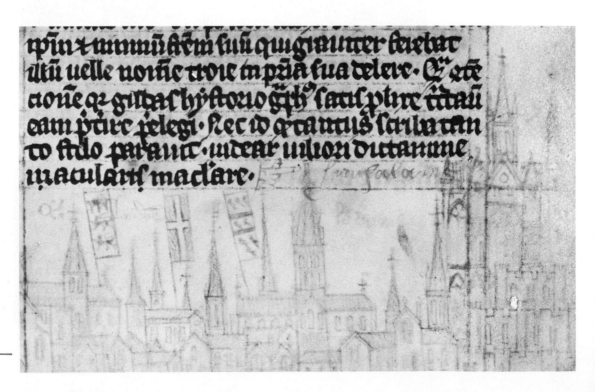

This drawing, squeezed into the lower margin of a book, represents London in the early fourteenth century. What do the buildings shown here tell you about the people of the time?

Document 2

Once a borough had been granted its charter, it was up to its citizens to work out a detailed *constitution* (a collection of rules and customs to be observed by the people and those in authority). The following extracts are taken from the constitution of Lincoln in about 1300.

> That the commonalty [community] shall by their common council elect a mayor. . . . And . . . with the advice of the mayor shall choose twelve . . . men to be judges. . . . And . . . four men worthy of trust shall be elected . . . to keep an account of outgoings, tallages [taxes] and arrears belonging to the city; and that they have one chest and four keys. . . . And that no person shall lodge a stranger more than one night unless he shall bring him forth to public view on the morrow if it shall be necessary. . . . Also it is provided that no foreign merchant shall remain in the city more than 40 days for selling his goods, unless he shall have licence of the mayor and commonalty . . . no foreign merchant of any kind of goods ought to be admitted to sell them within the city by retail [in a shop]. . . . Also it is forbidden that anyone shall exercise his rights in the common pastures but in a reasonable way as he ought, and that any hog shall be allowed to enter thereon to the injury of the pasture.

Adapted from J. J. Bagley, Historical Interpretation, *Penguin, 1965, pages 76–7*

Questions

1. Judging from this document, what sorts of things were particularly important to the people of Lincoln?
2. Why do you think four people were elected to look after Lincoln's finances, each with a key to the same chest?
3. Why do you think people were not allowed to give lodgings to strangers without being prepared to bring them out 'to public view'?
4. Can you explain the point of the rules controlling the activities of foreign merchants?

Stonemasons and carpenters in the thirteenth century working together on a building. Can you work out what each is doing and describe their tools? What things are done today in building a house which were not done in the Middle Ages?

Document 3

This is an extract from an Act of Parliament of 1388 dealing with the *sanitation* of towns (how they should be kept clean). It is believed to be the first of its kind in English history. (Entrails are intestines of animals; ordure is another word for dirt.)

For that so much Dung and Filth of the Garbage and Entrails as well of Beasts killed, as of other Corruptions, be cast and put in Ditches, Rivers and other Waters, and also within many other Places, within . . . Cities, Boroughs, and Towns of the Realm, and the suburbs of them, that the air there is greatly corrupt and infect, and many Maladies and other intolerable Diseases do daily happen. . . . It is assented [agreed] That Proclamation be made as well in the City of London, as in other Cities, Boroughs, and Towns through the Realm of England . . . that all they which do cast and lay all such Annoyances, Dung, Garbages, Entrails, and other Ordure in Ditches, Rivers, Waters, and other Places aforesaid, shall cause them utterly to be removed, avoided, and carried away betwixt this and the Feast of St. Michael next ensuing after the end of this present Parliament, every one upon Pain to lose and forfeit to our Lord the King £20.

Adapted from G. G. Coulton, Social Life in Britain, *C.U.P., 1918, pages 330–1*

Questions

1. Why had members of Parliament become concerned about this problem?
2. Why do you think the Act applies only to towns and cities?
3. Nowadays neither dung nor the carcases of dead animals are a threat to town sanitation. What changes since the fourteenth century have led to these improvements?
4. Why would it have been very hard for town dwellers at this time to obey the Act of 1388?

Document 4

Any member of a craft guild who broke its rules controlling the quality of goods for sale was liable to be punished. The records of the City of London for 1387 tell us what happened to a baker's servant who tried to trick customers.

Robert Porter, servant of John Gibbe, baker of Stratforde, was brought here, into the Guildhall of London, before Nicholas Extone, Mayor . . . and other Aldermen, and questioned for that, when the same Mayor on that day went into Chepe, to make assay there of bread, according to the custom of the City, he, the said Robert, knowing that the bread of his master, in a certain cart there, was not of full weight, took a penny loaf, and in it falsely and fraudulently inserted a piece of iron . . . And for this said falsity and deceit, it was adjudged that he should be taken from thence to Cornhulle, and be put upon the pillory there . . . for one hour of the day, the said loaf and piece of iron being hung about his neck. And precept [instruction] was given to the Sheriffs to have the reason for such punishment publicly proclaimed.

Quoted in G. G. Coulton, Social Life in Britain, *C.U.P., 1918, page 328*

Questions

1. What does it mean to 'make assay' of bread?
2. Why was it very important to people in those days that rules about the weight and quality of bread should be strictly enforced?
3. What happened when a wrongdoer was 'put upon the pillory'? Why would so much trouble have been taken to inform the public?
4. There is no mention of Robert's master, John Gibbe, being punished. Do you think this is fair? What might have been a suitable punishment for him?

Dress in the later Middle Ages

A peasant and his wife. Both wear simple tunics with shoes and belts of leather. Underneath, the wife wears a petticoat of linen or wool; her husband has woollen stockings which he rolls down in warm weather. Medieval clothes had no pockets, so pouches were necessary for carrying money and other small belongings

A nobleman and his wife. Over his close fitting doublet the noble wears a gown trimmed with fur. Shoes with long pointed toes were fashionable then. His wife's gown is called a houppelander and is made of silk. By law, only men and women of noble rank were allowed to wear the finest cloth and most costly furs. But these Sumptuary Laws were often broken by rich merchants and their wives, who liked to show off their wealth by dressing like nobles

THE BREAK-UP OF FEUDAL SOCIETY

BLACK DEATH AND PEASANTS' REVOLT

During the spring and summer of 1348 people in England lived in fear of a mysterious and unseen enemy. Merchants, seamen and travellers talked of a terrible plague that was spreading across Europe. It first appeared in the seaports of Sicily and Italy the previous autumn. Within a few months hundreds of thousands of men, women and children had died in Italy, Spain and France. With each new outbreak the plague moved nearer the British Isles.

The great plague

All over England people knelt in prayer or made pilgrimages to ask for deliverance. But while ships still crossed the Channel there was little chance of the Kingdom escaping infection. August came, and with it the dreaded plague – first reported in Dorset. Large swellings, some as big as apples, appeared under people's armpits and between their legs. These were quickly followed by black and blue blotches all over the body. Some people vomited and spat blood, their breath turning foul and stinking. Very few recovered from it. Within three days of being infected most sufferers were dead.

The 'Black Death', as some called it, was probably what modern doctors know as the *bubonic plague*. Even today it is a danger in parts of Asia. It is carried by fleas on the black rat (not the common brown rat, familiar in England) and can be passed on by the slightest contact with an infected person. The Black Death

Medicines being prepared. Many different kinds of herbs were used, along with less pleasant ingredients such as the insides of dead animals

Procession of monks in 1349 praying for deliverance from the Black Death

was first reported in China in 1334. So it probably reached Italy by means of rats on merchant ships carrying goods from the East.

The cause of the plague was discovered only about 100 years ago, so people in the fourteenth century had no idea how to prevent its spread. They knew nothing about germs and the link between dirt and disease. Some tried drinking vinegar, avoiding moist foods or bleeding themselves. Such 'remedies' seem ridiculous to us, but in the Middle Ages medical science was almost non-existent. Most people calling themselves doctors depended on guesswork and superstition. Patients were given medicines containing anything from crushed rocks to insects.

The plague soon spread throughout Britain. Dead bodies littered fields and roads all over the countryside. But the worst outbreaks were probably in the towns, where more people came into close contact. In London and other large towns cemeteries were quickly filled and fresh burial grounds had to be found. Deep trenches were dug and cartloads of corpses shovelled into them. Men were paid high wages for this work, because most people were afraid to go near plague victims.

By the end of 1350 the plague died down in England. Some writers of the time said it had killed half the people. The true figure was probably nearer a third – or well over one million people out of a total population of almost four million. The Black Death returned frequently in the years ahead. Many who lived through the first terrible outbreak were struck down when it reappeared in 1356, 1361–2 and 1368–9. But in time people must have developed some resistance to it, because most later outbreaks were mild in comparison with that of 1348.

Troubled times

The Black Death left its mark on England long after its victims had been buried in the ground. In some places whole villages were abandoned for lack of people to sow and reap the crops. Grass grew on the lanes and pathways, and deserted cottages fell into ruin. Lands once covered with carpets of corn were left to sprout weeds.

Before the Black Death, going as far back as the twelfth century, many villeins had been freed from their labour services to the lord of the manor. Instead of having to work part of the time on the lord's land they paid him rent for their cottage and strips. With this money the lord hired free labourers to work for wages. Most lords found that wage labourers worked harder than villeins who were always anxious to get back to their own strips.

After the plague, however, workers were scarce. Labourers realised their increased value and demanded more wages than before. Many lords paid up, rather than let their crops rot for lack of hands to gather them in. The same happened in the towns. Masters had to pay higher wages to get enough journeymen to work for them.

Parliament tried to put a stop to these demands. Laws were made ordering that wages should remain as they had been before the plague. But these were ignored, as a chronicler of the time, Henry Knighton, pointed out:

> The King proclaimed . . . that reapers and other labourers should not take more than they had been used to earning. . . . But the labourers were so sure of themselves and obstinate that they would not listen to the King's command . . . if anyone wished to employ them he would have to pay them what they wanted; he would either have to satisfy the greedy wishes of the workers or lose his fruit and crops.

With wages rising fast, those who were still villeins saw the increased advantages of being free-men. So they tried to exchange their labour services for money rents. Some lords agreed, but others refused to give villeins their freedom. They strictly enforced all labour services and made sure that slackers were fined in the manor court. Villeins became bitter and restless. The adventurous ones gathered their few possessions and fled, with their wives and children. They could easily find work in a town or on another manor. Workers were so hard to get that good wages were paid to newcomers and no questions asked about where they came from.

The common people of England, seeing the chance to better themselves, grew discontented with their lords and masters. There were threats of violence against some lords, including a number of abbots and bishops who refused to free their villeins. Because their estates belonged to the Church, many abbots and bishops claimed they should not rent them out or interfere with the old customs in any way. Villeins no longer accepted such excuses. They had lost respect for wealthy, pleasure-loving Church lords. So had many poor priests, who were firmly on the side of the peasants.

Ingarsby, in Leicestershire, was one of the many villages abandoned about the time of the Black Death. Hardly anything can be seen of it from the ground, but the places where houses once stood show up in this aerial photograph

The march to London

In the counties round London a travelling priest named John Ball stirred up the people against their lords. He attacked the greed of nobles and merchants and the idleness of many Church leaders. Ball said that things would not go well in England until there were no more lords to live off the sweat of the common people. In village after village men remembered his words:

> When Adam dalf [dug the ground] and Eve span,
> Who was thanne the gentilman?

Banned from preaching in churches, Ball went into the streets and market places, attracting large crowds. 'We are men formed in Christ's likeness,' he said, 'and they treat us like beasts.'

John Ball did more than preach. He and a group of determined followers plotted a rising of the common people. The seeds of revolt were beginning to grow when, in 1377, Richard II, a boy of ten, came to the throne. For a time the kingdom would have to be ruled by a council of nobles, most of them unpopular. Protests and gatherings of peasants and tradesmen were reported in several areas in 1377, 1378 and 1379.

Trouble came to a head when Parliament, meeting in November 1380, announced a *poll tax*. This was a tax on all people over the age of fifteen. The poor only had to pay fourpence, but this was more than a day's wages. When royal officials came to collect the tax many people hid themselves, so the amount gathered was much less than expected. In the spring of 1381 new officials were sent to root out the tax-dodgers and force them to pay.

In parts of Essex and Kent crowds drove away the tax-collectors and the 'Peasants' Revolt' had begun. In fact it was more than a revolt of peasants. Many tradesmen, parish priests, friars and outlaws joined in. On both sides of the Thames men took down

Richard II (1377–99). His father, Edward the 'Black Prince', was a great warrior. But Richard grew up to love books, music and art – not the sorts of interests that barons looked for in a king. After a troubled reign he ended up losing his throne and being murdered in a castle dungeon at the age of 33

scythes and sickles, sharpened axes and knives, or cleaned the swords and longbows they had fought with in France. Early in June the leaders met, at Maidstone in Kent, and chose a man named Wat Tyler to be their captain.

The rebels aimed to march to London and put their demands before the King, now aged fourteen. They had no quarrel with Richard himself. In fact they thought of him as their true leader. It was the council of nobles, the unpopular lords, tax-gatherers, lawyers and Church leaders who were in danger. As the armies from Essex and Kent swarmed towards London they attacked a number of manor houses and destroyed documents giving details of villeins' labour services. Prisoners were freed from jails – among them John Ball, whom the Archbishop of Canterbury had imprisoned at Maidstone.

By the evening of Wednesday 12 June the Essex men had camped in the fields of Mile End, just outside London. The men of Kent camped on Blackheath, five miles from London Bridge. We can only guess at their numbers, but there were probably at least 60,000 on both sides of the Thames. The King and his advisers took refuge in the Tower. Troops were on guard there, but they were not used. The rebel army was much too large to be crushed by force.

Wat Tyler meets the King

The rebel leaders sent word to Richard that they wished to speak with him. So next day the King and his advisers were rowed down the Thames towards Blackheath. But when the royal attendants saw the rebel forces face-to-face they refused to let the King land. The royal barges stopped and moved slowly away, to shouts and insults from those lining the river bank.

Tyler and the other leaders now decided to enter the City. No fighting was necessary. The common people of London opened the gates and welcomed the rebels. Across London Bridge streamed the men from Kent and other southern counties. Meanwhile the Essex men, with supporters from Hertfordshire, Suffolk and Cambridgeshire, marched in from the east, through Aldgate.

There were strict orders against looting and destruction. But first a few scores had to be settled. The prison in Fleet Street was broken open, the hated lawyers of the Temple were attacked, and the magnificent Savoy Palace, home of the King's uncle, John of Gaunt, was destroyed. Luckily for Gaunt, he was out of London at the time. From the Tower, Richard and his nobles saw the flames light up the night sky. The King would have to meet the rebels before it was too late.

Early next morning, Friday 14 June, Richard left the Tower with an escort of nobles and soldiers. As the jostling crowds struggled to catch a glimpse of him, he rode to Mile End, where Wat Tyler was waiting. Tyler came slowly forward on his pony, dismounted and kissed the royal hand. Then he put forward the peasants' demands, which included the abolition of feudal services, the renting of land at fourpence an acre, and the deaths of all 'traitors' to the people. Richard granted these requests, but added that only a court of law could decide whether a person was a traitor.

The peasants wanted proof of Richard's promises to take back to their lords. So thirty clerks set to work writing charters of freedom. Meanwhile, a band of rebels burst into the Tower. Inside they found Simon Sudbury, Archbishop of Canterbury, and royal ministers who had been responsible for the poll tax. They were all dragged to Tower Hill and beheaded. More executions of 'traitors' followed – mostly lawyers, tax-collectors and foreign merchants.

Once they had their charters many peasants went home. But the leaders stayed in London, still with a strong army, and another meeting with the King was arranged. This took place in the evening at Smithfield, a market and fair-ground. Again Tyler rode up on his pony and greeted Richard warmly. He demanded that lords' estates should be reduced to 'narrow proportions' and the lands of the Church should be divided among the people. Once more Richard agreed.

It was a hot day and Tyler called for a mug of water. He rinsed his mouth and spat on the ground. This may have seemed bad manners in front of a king, but by the standards of the time it was not unusual. As he mounted his pony, one of the King's followers shouted at him and a scuffle broke out. William Walworth, the Mayor of London, wounded Tyler, and a young squire finished him off. We shall never know whether it was Tyler's behaviour which caused the fight, or whether the royal attendants had planned to kill him.

When the rebels realised what had happened they drew back their bows. The royal party was in danger of being massacred, but Richard saved them. Spurring his horse towards the peasant ranks, he called out: 'Sirs, will you shoot your King? I am your captain, follow me.' Bewildered, but still trusting Richard, the people followed him into fields nearby. There he repeated his promises and talked them into going home. It was a triumphant moment for the young King.

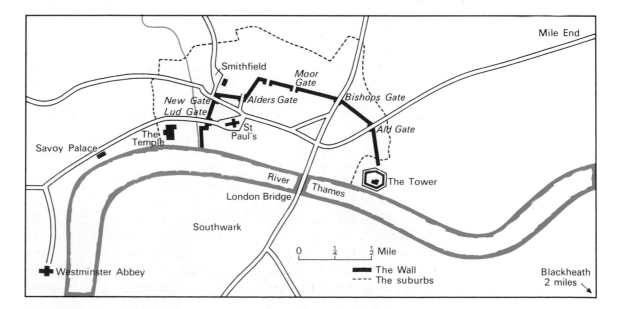

London at the time of the Peasants' Revolt

Work for the hangman

Once the rebels had been safely dispersed, the King and his council broke all the promises made at Mile End and Smithfield. Soldiers were gathered and any peasants left in London were arrested. Every householder in the City had to swear his loyalty to the King's government on a Bible. The next step was to put down the rising in the countryside and root out the ringleaders.

Royal forces went first into Essex, accompanied by the King and his judges. Everywhere the charters granted to villeins proved not to be worth the parchment they were written on. At Waltham, the King told a gathering of peasants: 'Villeins you were, and villeins you shall remain.' His forces moved through the county, putting down scattered attempts at resistance. In Chelmsford and Colchester, batches of rebel leaders were sentenced to death and hanged. In Kent too the roadside gallows soon creaked under the weight of rotting bodies.

In one form or another the rising spread as far north as York and as far west as Devon. But the main risings were in the south-eastern counties. The town of St Albans in Hertfordshire was on the estate of an abbey, and its citizens had long been refused the right to control their own affairs. On June 15 they ran riot, draining the abbot's fish-pond, killing the game in his woods and dividing his estate among themselves.

The abbot was forced to sign a borough charter, but soon afterwards a royal army arrived and the rebel leaders were rounded up and hanged. With them died John Ball. He had been captured in the Midlands and taken to St Albans for trial. Openly admitting his guilt, he went bravely to the gallows in the early morning light of July 15.

Bury St Edmunds, in Suffolk, was another town on the estates of an abbey, and the rising of 1381 was not the first in its unhappy history. Knowing the townsmen and peasants were after his

A fifteenth-century picture showing the execution of the Archbishop of Canterbury on Tower Hill. As he kneels (bottom left) his bishop's hat, or mitre, falls to the ground. This was later nailed to his skull when his head was stuck on London Bridge. The two who died with him were the King's Treasurer, Sir Robert Hales, and John Legge, organiser of the poll tax

John Ball, whose ideas did so
much to start the Revolt

The dramatic events at
Smithfield. In this fifteenth-
century picture, the artist has
combined two incidents in one.
On the left, Tyler is attacked
while Richard watches; on the
right the King rides towards the
rebel ranks.

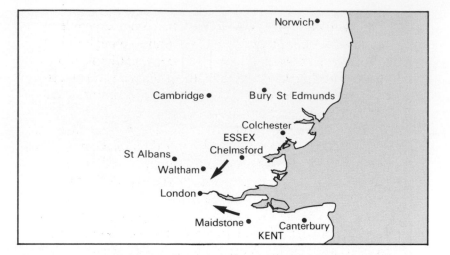

The trouble spots in south-eastern England, 1381

blood, the abbot fled. But he was hunted down and killed in a wood some miles away. His head was paraded round the town, together with that of the King's Chief Justice, Sir John Cavendish.

In the neighbouring county of Norfolk, the gates of Norwich were opened to a large rebel band. Peasants and tradesmen took over the castle and made knights wait on them at table! Not far away, at Cambridge, the people beheaded a judge and burned Corpus Christi, a college of the University which owned much property in the town. But here, as in other towns and villages, the rejoicing was short-lived. Troops arrived and soon there was more work for hangmen.

By the autumn the revolt had been completely crushed. On the surface it seemed the peasants had failed. But a rising as large and as well organised as that of 1381 was bound to leave its mark. Within ten years all attempts by Parliament to keep down wages were abandoned. And within fifty years nearly every lord had given up trying to force unwilling villeins to give labour services.

A gallows. All over south-east England in the summer and autumn of 1381 tattered figures swung from gallows like this

Sources and questions

1. Look at the picture on the lower half of page 197.
   (a) Which man is Wat Tyler? How can you tell?
   (b) Can you identify the mayor and the squire?
   (c) Why might the artist have made the King look much older than his actual age of fourteen?
   (d) Why did King Richard risk riding over to speak to the peasants alone?
   (e) Why do you think the peasants are made to look like a proper army? What do you think they would have looked like in real life and what weapons would they have carried?

2. The following extract is taken from the *Chronicle* of Jean Froissart, a Frenchman writing at the time of the Peasants' Revolt.

   It is the custom in England, as in other countries, for the

nobility to have great power over the common people, who are . . . bound by law and custom to plough the fields of their masters, harvest the corn, gather it into barns, and thresh and winnow the grain; they must also mow and carry home the hay, cut and collect wood, and perform all manner of tasks. . . .

The wretched peasantry . . . now began to rebel, saying that . . . at the beginning of the world no man was a slave; nor ought anyone to be treated as such. . . . This they would no longer endure: if they were to work for their masters then they must be paid. . . .

A mad priest in the county of Kent, John Ball by name, had for some time been encouraging these notions, and had several times been confined in the Archbishop of Canterbury's prison for his absurd speeches. For it was his habit . . . to collect a crowd . . . and address them more or less as follows: 'My friends, the state of England cannot be right until . . . there is no distinction between nobleman and serf, and we are all as one. . . . They are dressed in velvet and furs, while we wear only cloth. They have wine, and spices and good bread, while we have rye . . . and water to drink. They have fine houses and manors, and we have to brave the wind and rain as we toil in the fields. . . . Let us go to the King. He is young, and we will show him our miserable slavery; we will tell him it must be changed, or else we will provide the remedy ourselves.

Froissart's Chronicles, *Book 1, edited and translated by John Jolliffe, Harvill Press, 1967, pages 236–8*

(a) Where in this passage does Froissart appear to take sides?

(b) What evidence can you find in this passage that the writer had some sympathy with the plight of the peasants?

(c) According to Froissart, what was the peasants' main aim? How would the effects of the Black Death have made them all the more determined to achieve their aim?

(d) Why do you think the peasants trusted King Richard II to treat them fairly?

(e) Imagine you were a lord living at this time. How would you defend your way of life and privileges against the arguments of John Ball?

3. In the form of a diary, describe the Peasants' Revolt from the point of view of an Essex or Kent man who marched to London and was present at Wat Tyler's death.

4. 'Wat Tyler let victory slip from his fingers.' If you had been the peasants' leader, in complete control of London, what would you have done to make sure Richard's promises were kept? (Why do you think such schemes did not occur to Wat Tyler?)

THE HUNDRED YEARS WAR

Effigy of Edward III (1327–77) in Westminster Abbey. He was the kind of warrior king that nobles respected and were keen to follow into battle. He loved the excitement of war and the glory of victory. Although he fought against the King of France, Edward was himself half French by birth and spoke French more easily than English

The kings of England had ruled lands on both sides of the Channel since the Norman Conquest of 1066. In the twelfth century, Henry II controlled more than half of France. But the French kings aimed to drive out their English rivals. Nearly all the lands Henry ruled were soon lost – most of them in the reign of his son, the unfortunate John.

When Edward III became king of England, in 1337, only the provinces of Gascony and Guienne remained in English hands (see map on page 203). These were important wine producing areas. Every year thousands of casks of French wine were shipped from Bordeaux to London, Bristol and Southampton. English merchants and nobles feared that this profitable trade might be spoilt if the French king conquered Gascony and Guienne. They urged Edward III to fight to keep these territories.

Edward, who enjoyed fighting, needed no encouragement. His mother was a French princess and he claimed he had more right to the French throne than Philip VI (1328–50). Philip was a cousin of the previous king whereas Edward was a nephew. The French nobles did not want Edward, and he must have realised he had little chance of getting the crown of France. But if he was successful in battle at least Gascony and Guienne would be safe, and he might gain other lands too.

After lengthy arguments between the two kings, Edward declared war in 1337. It was the start of a long series of raids and English invasions, with intervals of peace in between, which lasted until 1453. We call it the 'Hundred Years War', although the actual fighting amounted to much less than 100 years.

The badge of the present-day Grand National Archery Society, showing a longbowman of about the year 1400. Notice he had a metal breastplate buckled over his jerkin. His longbow, made of springy yew, elm or hazelwood, had a tough string of hemp or linen. Arrows were tipped with iron and feathered with quills from geese, turkeys or swans

Edward III's army

During his Welsh and Scottish campaigns, Edward III's grandfather, Edward I, had found the old feudal method of raising an army unsatisfactory. He often needed long periods of service from his troops and tighter control over them, so he employed more and more 'regular' soldiers who were paid wages. Such recruiting was done by means of *indentures* – agreements between the Crown

English longbowmen practising. The targets, banked up with mounds of earth, were called butts

and trusted commanders who promised to raise and equip a certain number of soldiers to fight, at home or abroad, for as long as required.

The commanders of the king's army made their own indentures with the soldiers they recruited. A clerk wrote out the details of each agreement twice on a single sheet of parchment. He then made a zig-zag cut between the two copies, giving one copy to the commander and one to the soldier. This was proof of the agreement, because the irregular edges of an indenture would fit together – like upper and lower sets of teeth, which is how such documents got their name.

By Edward III's time, there were fewer knights on horseback and many more archers and other footsoldiers in the king's army. Archers used the longbow – the deadly weapon Edward I had found so effective in his Scottish wars. They wore iron caps, stout leather jackets, and sometimes a short sword hung from their belts as well as a quiver of arrows. Few longbowmen were poor peasants. Most were freemen; usually either town tradesmen or small farmers who rented their own land. It took great skill to shoot a longbow accurately, so regular practice was essential.

Edward's knights, carrying shields and lances or swords, were much more heavily armoured than those of earlier centuries. Over their coats of mail, most knights now wore specially shaped pieces of plate armour on the chest, knees, elbows, feet and other parts of the body. Hands were covered with iron gauntlets, and the helmet protected the whole head, with a *visor* (small hinged cover) over the face.

A full set of plate armour was so heavy that if a knight was knocked off his horse he was barely able to defend himself. He might be killed or captured if there was no one near to help him escape. Over his armour a knight wore a linen tunic, or surcoat, with his family's coat-of-arms embroidered on it. This was the only sure way of recognising him on the battlefield.

To get an army across the Channel, complete with horses, siege towers and all the equipment of cooks, blacksmiths and other necessary tradesmen, Edward needed a large fleet of ships. He could afford to keep only a few ships of his own. The rest were hired from merchants. The so-called 'Cinque Ports' of Dover, Romney, Sandwich, Hastings and Hythe had a special duty to

DOCUMENTS: THE KING'S ARMY AND THE FRENCH WARS

Document 1

An especially valuable source on the Hundred Years War up to the end of the fourteenth century is the *Chronicle* of Jean Froissart. Although a Frenchman by birth, he tried to report events fairly and was excited by the brave and honourable deeds of the nobles on both sides. This is part of Froissart's account of the sea-battle of Sluys (1340), which occurred when he was a child.

> King Edward . . . drew up his ships in line so that there was one shipload of men-at-arms between every two of archers. . . . There were on board a large number of noble ladies on their way to Ghent to attend the Queen. . . . They were well escorted by three hundred men-at-arms and five hundred archers, provided by the King. . . .
>
> A fierce battle broke out, each side opening fire with cross-bows and longbows, and hand-to-hand fighting began. The soldiers used grappling irons on chains in order to come to grips with the enemy boats. . . .
>
> Sea-battles are always more terrible than those on land, for those engaged can neither retreat nor run away; they can only stand and fight to the bitter end, and show their courage and endurance. . . . The battle lasted from early in the morning till noon, and in that time the English were hard pressed. . . . But they fought so valiantly . . . that they won the day. Their enemies were all killed or drowned, and not one escaped.

Froissart's Chronicles, *Book 1, edited and translated by John Jolliffe, Harvill Press, 1967, pages 103–4*

Questions

1. What evidence is there in this account that the English did not expect to be defeated at sea?
2. Why did the English King prepare for the battle by lining up shiploads of archers and men-at-arms alternately? How was this suited to the method of fighting?
3. Froissart was inclined to exaggerate. Can you find a clear example in this extract?
4. Imagine you are an English archer who has just survived the battle of Sluys. Write a letter home explaining why, in Froissart's words, sea-battles are 'more terrible than those on land'.

This fifteenth-century drawing of a sea-fight in the Channel shows one ship ramming another while the crews fight at close quarters. What weapons are being used by the soldiers? In the future, how would weapons using gunpowder begin to change fighting methods at sea and make them less like those on land?

Document 2

The following document, which is dated 22 March 1347, speaks for itself. (Michaelmas, which means the feast of St Michael, is on 29 September.)

> This indenture, made between our lord Edward king of England and of France and lord of Ireland of the one part and Henry Husee of the other part, witnesses that the said Henry has undertaken the defence of the Isle of Wight until next Michaelmas with forty men-at-arms and sixty archers at the king's expense. He will begin to be responsible for these same men and for the island immediately after Easter, and he will be paid wages for the said men at a rate agreed between himself and the treasurer of our lord the king.
>
> In witness of this, our said lord the king holds the part of this indenture concerning the said Henry, and the said Henry holds the other part of the same indenture concerning our said lord the king. And they have attached their seals.

Quoted in J. J. Bagley, Historical Interpretation, *Penguin, 1965, page 148*

Questions

1. Why are the King and Henry Husee each described as holding a 'part' of the indenture? How were such documents designed to prevent forgery?
2. What method of recruiting an army did indentures of this kind replace, and for what reasons?
3. A hundred men is not a large force. What had happened a few years before to reduce the risk of an enemy attack in this region?
4. Why do you think Edward's titles include the kingship of France? How far was this an accurate description in 1347?

This indenture – made between the Earl of Chester and Lincoln and the men of Frieston and Butterwick – dates from the early thirteenth century. Why and how were seals attached to such documents? Why are there so many seals on this one?

*German printing press –
from a book published in
the sixteenth century*

and upbringing but also by three different languages. Latin was written and spoken by scholars and churchmen; most books were in Latin, and its grammar was the basis of all education. After the Norman Conquest, French-speaking kings and lords ruled England, and only the peasants and tradesmen of Saxon stock spoke English.

Even among common folk, however, there was not one English tongue but many, for there were dozens of *dialects* (varieties of the same language). Strong traces of these remain today, but in the Middle Ages it was often impossible for people from different parts of the country to understand each other.

French died out very slowly in England. It was not until Edward III's reign (1327–77) that English became the chief language of the royal court and of Parliament. By then many French words, and Latin ones too, had blended with the Old English. It was a richer language, usually offering a choice of words with similar meanings. For example, today Old English words such as great, small and begin have French-based alternatives: grand, petty and commence.

A well-known figure in Edward III's court was the poet Geoffrey Chaucer (see Chapter 13). His *Canterbury Tales* and other works were written in English. They were greatly admired and other poets tried to copy Chaucer's style. Consequently the form of English spoken by Chaucer and the people of London gradually came to be understood by educated men in other parts of the country. It was an important step towards a common English language.

Copies of Chaucer's poems, handwritten on parchment, were hard to come by and very expensive – as were all books in the Middle Ages. But this was soon to change, because in the middle of the fifteenth century a printing press was invented in Germany. John Gutenberg, a citizen of Mainz, is thought to have produced the first printed book, soon after 1450. Previously it had only been possible to 'block print' pictures carved on wood. But the German press had movable type, so pages of writing could be set up. The craft of paper-making had recently come to Europe from the East, and this, together with printing, made books a lot cheaper.

Knowledge of printing was brought to England by William Caxton, a wealthy English merchant who lived for many years in Bruges, a town in the Netherlands. Caxton enjoyed collecting books and translating French works into English, carefully copying them out himself. When he heard about the invention of printing in Germany he went there to study the new craft. Later he constructed a press in Bruges, where in 1475 he printed the first books in English.

Caxton brought his press to London in the following year and set up a workshop near the Palace of Westminster. In the remaining fifteen years of his life he printed copies of nearly 100 different

William Caxton, 1422–91

Part of the Prologue to The Canterbury Tales, *taken from one of the earliest printed editions, 1485*

The coronation of Elizabeth II in 1953. Many parts of the ceremony date from the Middle Ages

In 1453, while the Hundred Years War was ending in France, a dramatic event took place on the other side of the Continent. The great city of Constantinople was besieged and finally captured by Muslim Turks. The thousand-year-old Byzantine Empire was no more. Some of its finest scholars had already fled to Italy, where their knowledge helped to bring new ways of life and thought in the West. The fall of Constantinople was therefore both an end and a beginning.

The scholars of Constantinople had preserved the learning of ancient Greece. In a similar way, people today keep alive medieval customs and beliefs, often without realising it. All over Europe men and women worship in medieval churches and cathedrals, while the Catholic Church is still the largest of all the Christian communities. Most people live in towns and villages that were settled and named in the Middle Ages. Even the names of the people themselves often remind us of medieval trades and occupations.

In Britain we still have kings and queens, and they are crowned at Westminster in much the same way as William the Conqueror and his successors were. We still have the two Houses of Parliament. In the Lords the Chancellor sits on the Woolsack, a reminder of the great medieval industry; and in the Commons M.P.s grant taxes just as knights and burgesses did long ago. Our local government of councils and mayors has its roots in the Middle Ages. And the same is true of the law courts, with their juries of twelve ordinary men and women. Moreover, the judges wear medieval robes and travel round the counties as Henry II's justices did over 800 years ago.

The people of modern Britain can create electricity from nuclear energy, feed their problems to computers and fly round the world much faster than Chaucer's pilgrims could ride to Canterbury. But they have kept their medieval traditions in law and government – and they are proud to have them. When foreign tourists come to Britain, these are the things they are most eager to see.

Sources and questions

1. Look at the picture of printing on page 214.
   (a) What are the two people by the window doing?
   (b) What is the job of the man in front on the right?
   (c) Describe what the other man in front needs to do to print the next sheet. Why was the machine called a press?
   (d) In addition to the processes shown in the picture, what else needed to be done to produce a book?
   (e) Explain the main difference between the method of printing shown in the picture and the way in which the picture itself would have been printed.

2. This is part of an introduction William Caxton wrote for one of his printed books which he translated himself from French into English. It has been left in the original spelling.

   > And that comyn englysshe that is spoken in one shyre [county] varyeth from another. In so moche that in my dayes happened that certayn marchauntes [merchants] were in a shippe in Tamyse [river Thames] . . . and wente to lande for to refreshe them; And one of theym . . . cam in-to an hows and axed for mete; and specyally he axyed after eggys; and the goode wyf answerde, that she coude speke no frensshe. And the marchaunt was angry, for he also coude speke no frensshe, but wolde hauc hadde 'egges' and she vunderstode hym not. And theene at laste another sayd that he wolde haue 'eyren' then the good wyf sayd that she vnderstod hym wel. Loo, what sholde a man in thyse dayes now wryte, 'egges' or 'eyren'?

   Quoted in G. M. Trevelyan, Illustrated English Social History, *Volume 1, Longman, 1949, page 78*

   (a) Why would this kind of misunderstanding have interested a man like Caxton?
   (b) When the woman heard a word she did not understand, why do you think she automatically thought it was French?
   (c) What do you think was Caxton's purpose in telling this story in a book he had translated into English?
   (d) How would the work of Caxton and other printers help to reduce this kind of misunderstanding in the future?

3. (a) Modern methods of printing are very different from those in Caxton's day. Do you know how printing is done without using a 'press' of any kind?
   (b) Make a list of all the things that would be different today if printing had never been invented.

4. If you had to plan a tour for foreign visitors interested in the medieval history of Britain, what *ten* places would you pick out to show them, and why?

INDEX